I KNOW WHAT THE
RED CLAY LOOKS LIKE

I KNOW WHAT THE RED CLAY LOOKS LIKE

—

THE VOICE AND VISION

of

BLACK WOMEN WRITERS

—

by

REBECCA CARROLL

CAROL SOUTHERN BOOKS
NEW YORK

PHOTOGRAPHS BY:

Davida Adedjouma: Kathleen/Vernon G. May
Tina McElroy Ansa: Jonée Ansa
Lorene Cary: George R. Johnson
Pearl Cleage: Barry Forbus
J. California Cooper: Melvin Terry
Rita Dove: Fred Viebahn
Gloria Wade Gayles: William H. Ransom
Marita Golden: George de Vincent
June Jordan: Haruko
Gloria Naylor: Marion Ettinger
Barbara Neely: Marilyn Humphries
Gwen Parker: Lorin Klaris
Charlotte Watson Sherman: Ted M. Kelly
Barbara Summers: Coreen Simpson

Copyright © 1994 by Rebecca Carroll

A complete listing of permissions to reprint previously published material begins on page vi.

All rights reserved. No part of this book may be reproduced or transmitted in any form or by any means, electronic or mechanical, including photocopying, recording, or by any information storage and retrieval system, without permission in writing from the publisher.

Published by Carol Southern Books in hardcover and by Crown Trade Paperbacks, both imprints of Crown Publishers, Inc., 201 East 50th Street, New York, New York 10022. Member of the Crown Publishing Group.

Random House, Inc.   New York, Toronto, London, Sydney, Auckland

Carol Southern Books and colophon and Crown Trade Paperbacks and colophon are trademarks of Crown Publishers, Inc.

Manufactured in the United States of America

Library of Congress Cataloging-in-Publication Data
Carroll, Rebecca
    I know what the red clay looks like : the voice and vision of
Black American women writers / by Rebecca Carroll. — 1st ed.
        p.   cm.
    1. American literature—Afro-American authors—History and criticism—Theory, etc.
2. American literature—20th century—History and criticism—Theory, etc.   3. Women and
literature—United States—History—20th century.   4. Afro-American women authors—
20th century—Interviews.   5. Afro-American women in literature.   6. Afro-Americans in
literature.   I. Title.
PS153.N5C375   1994
810.9'9287'08996073—dc20
                                                                                94-8342
                                                                                CIP

ISBN 0-517-59638-5
ISBN 0-517-88261-2—pbk.
10   9   8   7   6   5   4   3   2   1
First Edition

For

Monique Cormier, my soul mate and life organizer, whose faith in me has been unyielding, and without whose emotional support this project would not have been possible

ACKNOWLEDGMENTS

Grateful acknowledgment for financial, moral, and divine support to my parents, Laurette and David Carroll; Mother Jan; The Girlfriends—Rebecca Emeny, Laura Donovan, Wini Dean, and Elaine Hackney; my agent, Meredith Bernstein; my publisher, Carol Southern, and my generous and gracious editor, Eliza Scott; Bob Coles, Les Fisher, Michael Ladd, Florence Ladd, and Eleanor Cawthorne; Steve Welch, Loren Hill, and Agnes Burke.

There is no appropriate thanks for the writers who lent their souls, pledged a sacred day to me, in honor of this project. The range of senses, the power of Being, standing tall behind words written for themselves, for others, for joy. Black Women sing in this book; they sing a song composed for and by each other. I am tremendously grateful to have been in the choir, if only orchestrating the music—their tenor, soprano, and alto voices came forward at my behest, deep, resilient, and passionate. Their voices are the lifeblood of each living page.

CONTENTS

AUTHOR'S NOTE

I Know What the Red Clay Looks Like is a collection of interviews with black women writers. Although I did indeed conduct interviews with these writers, asked them questions, and listened intently to their answers in a crowded New York City café, or a quiet, sweet-smelling sunroom, or a dark, tea-colored office in the back of a small studio, each interview evolved into a conversation. And the conversation was about words: how we use them and how our black womanness inspires, encourages, and pushes those words across a blank page, time and time again. Each writer in the book boldly and soulfully discussed with me her opinions, politics and emotions, her style, each in unique and provocative ways, all the while absolutely exuding her sense of self as a Black Woman Writer.

I began the book with the impetus of Audre Lorde's essay on "The Erotic." Lorde spoke of "The Erotic" as a resource; the feeling of balance between our sense of self and the chaos of our strongest feelings, about everything. She went on further to say that once this feeling is recognized, we are creatively empowered to claim our voices, our histories, our work, and our lives. My feeling is that the quickest route to this erotic resource is by allowing ourselves to be the sensual beings that we are—to genuinely listen, touch, speak, hear, and taste our experiences. These experiences captured in the written word are powerful and invaluable, because they at once become part of someone else's experience—she, or he, who reads them.

The title of this book is of course a reference to the red clay in Georgia, it having one of the richest colors and most authentic textures there is. I feel as though black women writers have been just as rich in color and authentic in texture for some time now.

We have created a room of our own, and it is gorgeous. In this book, we continued to paint its walls with the even strokes of our collective vocal rhythms.

By the end of *I Know What the Red Clay Looks Like*, I started to think that writing was a very female medium—a woman-art, a talent that required hips. But writing is a way of thinking, of being, of figuring things out, with or without hips. Choosing to consider yourself as a writer—accepting the challenge of taking the word from its most natural modus operandi, on the lips, in the air, between two people, putting it on a page, where it may sit, dark and motionless, and then creating movement around it so that it comes alive and speaks in another way, to me, is tremendous. The different ways in which blackness resonates through writing has caused me to fall in love with what I do. And that is to give rise to the voice of black literature.

My experiences with these writers, with this book, and with my own writing have made me wake up in the morning wearing a sleep that I do not recognize. Although I feel strangely stirred by it. Throughout any given day, the air I breathe has a peculiar taste, almost like nectar, but more like honey. On the same day, my eyes will ache, an ache that one might feel from seeing something astoundingly beautiful, and all I can make of the pain is a very poignant image of smooth, scorching black skin. When the evening comes, as I sense the beginning again of a sleep I do not know, I feel warmth in a woman's voice. She is telling a story. A story she said I had asked to hear . . .

We talked about words.
How they curl
around our tongues.
Black words.
Female words.
Real words.

We talked about language.
How it becomes
life,
love,
song,
dance,
The Get Down.

We talked about soul.
How it hurts,
laughs,
sleeps,
whispers.

We talked about history.
How it has become

our own,
after years of it belonging to
them,
him,
anyone,
but Us.

Our history.
Yes.
That We made.
With our words,
our language,
our souls,
our hips,
and our blood.
Blood the color of red clay.

Did you ever wonder
How
that clay got red?

—Rebecca Carroll
November 30, 1993

DAVIDA
ADEDJOUMA

D

AVIDA ADEDJOUMA is wife, mother, grandmother, soothsayer, and any and everything else in between. Born in Chicago in 1956, she has spent most of her adult life in Minnesota. A novelist and short-story writer, Davida has received a Bush Individual Artist Fellowship, a Jerome Travel-and-Study Grant, and a Minnesota State Arts Board Career Opportunity Grant, all of which afforded her the opportunity to live and write in Paris for an extended time, where she and her husband maintain a studio. She teaches creative writing in community programs and is the owner of Creative Consultations, a writing/media relations agency. Her collection of short stories, *Last Summer* (New Rivers Press), was a winner of the 1987 Minnesota Voices Competition. She is currently finishing work on a novel, *The Myth Makers*.

WRITE FOR THE SAME REASON I breathe, eat, sleep, make love, form friendships and relationships . . . dare to begin new ones, sometimes speak when I should listen, sometimes retreat when I should attack, mother, care-take, and love—to stay alive.

Words and I have a monogamous relationship. We met when I was about three. My mother taught me how to read by reading to me every night. For about six months one time I made her read *The Wizard of Oz* every night. Every single night I had to hear that story because I wanted a tornado to take me off somewhere. I never felt like I was supposed to be living where I was. There had to be another world. I honestly believed a tornado had transported Dorothy to Oz and that she'd had marvelous, dangerous adventures. I went to sleep dreaming—my way of praying in those days—of the power to use words. Soon, I started to write.

After I had my son, Charlie, at nineteen, I couldn't seem to do too much of anything, couldn't get my act together. I just thought, "Well, you blew it." Single mother, black, fat, and on welfare in Minnesota? I figured I would die early. I couldn't even think. I played bingo for ten years and actually made more money at bingo than I've made doing anything else. I would watch soaps all day, read all night, play bid whist on the weekend. My friends could never understand the reading part—the soaps they could get, but not the reading. Eventually, I went back to college and occasionally worked, even though I have a hard time with the routine boredom of nine-to-five jobs.

When I started writing on a regular basis, Charlie would wait until I had been at it for a couple of days, and then he'd say, "Mom, you think you should take a bath, and maybe comb your hair, and can we go out to eat?" Sometimes I would honestly forget he was there. He knew I was there for him, but he also knew when I had to write. Part of it was that I needed something that was mine alone so badly. I needed my own room. I needed to do what I wanted to do because I'd grown up doing what everybody else wanted me to do.

I felt like I was a writer when *Last Summer* was published. I'd written most of the book during the period following a closed-head injury and later breakdown. My "loony" period. Part of my therapy included keeping a journal. That's when I wrote "Bingo." The insurance company covering my therapy paid for me to take a creative writing class because they figured—hell, I had been on workman's compensation for four years, I may as well do something. So I took a writing class at the downtown post office in St. Paul. All of the stories in the book, except "Heaven vs. Hell," were homework assignments. When the book was going to the printer, my editor said, "I don't have time to edit anything else. This one story doesn't work; you're just going to have to write something new." I sat down and wrote "Heaven vs. Hell," and it went in just the way I wrote it.

"Heaven vs. Hell" was my response to my brief stint working for the Minnesota Coalition for Battered Women. I'd see these women, hear their stories, and I'd think—"Look, if you're gonna sit up there and be beat anyway, the least you can do is let this man know you been *in* his ass, too, 'cause I'll be damned if some man hit me." My father never hit me, I cannot see any other man hitting me. I have tried to imagine the situation, especially being married now, and I think about my husband—I love the man dearly, but if he ever hit me, we're not going to counseling. There's nothing to counsel about—either I'm gonna lay him out, or he's gonna lay me out, and that's gonna be the end of it. Some man beatin' on me? No, uh-uh. So that's what "Heaven vs. Hell" was about.

I hate reviews, even though almost all of them were good and no, I still don't plot well. But I'm still angry with the first woman who was going to review the book for a newspaper here. She came out to my house—now, naturally it was Black History Month— and so here I am, the first black woman writer to win the competition, which resulted in the book's publication. This woman comes out to my house and tells my son, with the most condescending voice possible, "Now pose with your mom the way you do when she's writing." I'm like—wait a minute. First of all, what would make her think I can write with my child hanging over my shoulder?

Then we talked, you know, interview-type junk, and I asked her what she thought of the book, since we had yet to talk about it. She said, "Well, I didn't really understand it, and I'm not sure white readers will know what you're talking about, but the last story showed that you *might* be able to write." I said, "If you can't understand it, then why are you reviewing it?" She was quiet, and I was like, "This isn't a book review, this is finding something to write about for Black History Month, and if you print the shit the way you plannin' on printin' it, I'm gonna write a rebuttal." She never ran the story. My publisher told me I couldn't go around making enemies of book reviewers, and I said, "Shoot! The bitch ain't got nothin' I need." I don't know why I was surprised, this *is* Minnesota, and there wasn't a cabin up north, a fish or a farm in it.

I get really tired of the way race gets played out in America. Particularly in the arts. Who controls the image? What is the valid story? When I moved to Paris in 1987, it was because I wanted to explore the whole notion of it being easier to make it in Paris as a black American artist than it is here. I was in Paris for two years, with basically no money, and I survived without losing any sense of dignity. I could not be writing what I am writing now if I had not gone to Paris. I didn't feel like I wasn't living up to anybody's expectations, or even that I *had* to live up to anybody's expectations. If somebody asked me what I did, I said I wrote. Period.

Here I get it from all directions: it's not black enough; there's too much dialogue. Damn it, it's my story and I'm going to tell it the way I want to. But I can write when I'm angry. I've been angry enough since I've been back in the States to write a whole lot. It's funny because when I went back to Paris just recently for the 1992 Afro-American Writers Conference, I read from my work in progress (it was writing that I had done after coming back from Paris the first time). And my agent, who was also at the conference, said to me, "Look, here in Paris you are living the story too much, go back to the States, finish this book and then come back to live." And that is exactly what it feels like. I can write in the States, but to live, I can't be here.

The one very positive thing about this country is the black women writers who are here, who have really inspired me. Gloria Naylor has been extremely supportive of me. I wrote to her after I read *Linden Hills*, and she wrote me back right away. Then when my book came out, I sent her a copy, and she has been real encouraging of my writing ever since. We didn't actually meet until after three years of writing to each other. Gwendolyn Brooks has also been very inspirational. I went to an all-black private school, and I got a chance to meet her. That was the first time I learned that black women were writers, and so of course I could be a writer. Gayl Jones hits hard. And nobody will ever touch Zora Neale Hurston's *Their Eyes Were Watching God*. Toni Morrison is a "sentence goddess," Colleen McElroy a spellbinder. I wish that

Nella Larsen had kept writing. I think what really strikes me about black women writers is that we are all writing the same love story.

Right now I feel we are developing a language for what we are, where we are going, and who we are as a community of black women. And there is a tremendous amount of sexuality and sensuality within that community. The claiming of black women's sexuality and sensuality by black women writers comes from the strength of our own togetherness, and the courage of putting that experience on paper. Our experience as black women, as sexual and sensual beings, has been defined for us for so long, almost to the point where we don't even know what it is.

The language that we are now creating to set the record straight is loud, and it will not be developed out of any blanket feminism, because there is so much commercial feminism that has nothing to do with black women that is also just as patriarchal as anything else in this society. I really don't want any white woman to tell me how to spell the word *women*. My name is what my name is, and no one can tell me how to spell it. I hate someone defining my sexuality to me. *Especially* my sexuality. If anyone is going to control it, I'm going to control it. There is a unique power in black women's sexuality, it's not about sex, and when it finally gets dealt with honestly, it *will* be powerful. Black women writers are opening that door, hands clasped together, and walking right on through it.

Writing is keeping me alive. If I stop, I'm afraid of what will happen. It saves my sanity, because I can go as insane as I want to in the writing, and I don't worry about the punctuation, and I don't go through a bunch of changes. I simply put it down on paper and where I come up for air I stick a comma. When I go to the state fair, there is this one ride that I always go on. It has this safety bar because the ride flips upside down. And every time I'm on that ride, high up in the air, I start rattling the safety bar, because I want to know what it would feel like if the bar dropped. But it never drops. I have rattled it, I have sat on the very corner edge, figuring that just my sheer weight ought to make the bar drop. But it never does. That is the sensation I get when I am writing—that slow pull upward, and then . . . I will probably go to the fair again this year.

From
THE MYTH MAKERS
In the Still of Night

"My name is Kyle.

"I walk these streets slickened by leaves pooling in clots of red, red-gold and burnt sienna congealing like spilled blood on this street where the air is a pneumatic cough, a wheeze of dry-rot, wet paper, burnt meals and aspirations gone sour. Buildings here edge toward collapse and totter; and the streets narrow, forcing me to dodge the tangled legs of sweet winos who lounge on the sidewalk drinking, winking, and nodding against walls grey as forgotten corners. The streets narrow, propelling me toward the envy of the exhausted who, in thigh-high skirts and low-cut shirts, lean against open doorways selling sticky-sweet moments of fumbled pleasure on rough-dried sheets; and their stiletto heels click *me . . . pick me . . . pick me* as they walk. I walk these streets where there's a contagious lack of energy as even the streetlights fffsst off . . . then on . . . offon, offon mellow as the glow of fireflies.

"I walk in the evening, when the night is still; and at the hour of the oohhing women *aahh* the women seduced by slow vowels, swallowed consonants, the game of delusion begins: fuck me, love me not . . . come! Walk with me to the ledge of night where a woman shivers while cradling a child as dark-skinned and dark-haired and dark-eyed as the one rounding her belly will be. Swaddled in scarves faded as a velveteen sofa, the child cries a haunting melody wanting more than our coins, needing more than the angel of Sèvres-Babylone who closes her eyes and plucks love songs with short pudgy fingers: a wallflower who knows the steps but no one has ever asked her to dance.

"We won't stop fifty feet from the station where on sunny days or for special customers a humming woman still pricks her finger threading the needle and does the beading by hand, sewing traces of blood and a secret gold thread into the fabric. That day I shuffled until my question was absorbed by the cards, then cut to my left three times with my left hand and she told me. 'You'll find, in your future, all roads lead back home.'

"We'll rush pass the cemetery where a grave is still fresh and a fat orange cat with white toes and white on the tip of her nose prowls anxious as a memory.

"Come, follow me down that street of happiness where lying in the gutter like a broken glass slipper is a single black pump, its t-strap unraveling, its heel run-over on this street of happiness where there's something luxurious in the anonymous existence of women *aahh* women in diamonds and furs, vacationing women who say yes when they need it, no when they don't.

"Come follow me to the impasse of gaiety.

"There's a heavy locked door but I know the code to this Eden of anorexic branches tapping at the window of a ground floor studio baptized in urine and ten drops of sugar, a dark tilted womb where love grows lean, fragile as a membrane, and where promises made in the still of night were broken. Here sunlight seeps through a dingy mesh curtain; and the bathroom sink is a wounded flamingo wobbling on a broken steel leg. Spiders web the ceiling, silverfish swim along the faded design of the carpet. Forgotten on the closet shelf, hidden from sight, is a silver dime, an old, old penny, a pinch of bread, a clove of garlic. And Jesus hangs on the wall, head bowed.

"I come here because he's here, they tell me to *let him go.*

"And I would if I could but I remember the night he kissed my neck, my left nipple, my right, then his tongue warm inside me doing what the nasty boys wouldn't; the night I grabbed his hair screaming love me, fuck me not, no! I don't know why he bit my ear till I cried warm blood warm as the breath of the first woman who asked me to dance the night I should have known, but didn't, yet, but should have known because it was Niagara who invited me to the club, Niagara who said, 'Can Kyle come out and play?' Then she winked. What did she see in me? The night I entered the club Niagara was spinning an extended version of what I didn't dare and then this woman: her baby hair wasn't white-girl straight, her kitchen-hair wasn't black girl nappy it was the kind of hair which, if she would just sit between her legs, tilt her head into my thighs, I could part in four equal sections, massage coconut oil into her scalp, electrifying the air between us. *Just us.* Because three at a head the middle one's dead so it would just be the two of us and I'd brush, one-thousand. Two, one-thousand. Three, one-thousand brush four until my hand ached. And she would purr. Deeply, because she wouldn't be tender-headed. Contentedly, because I'm not heavy-handed: I'd plait her hair under and over, under and over precise as haiku then we'd rub the loose strands between our hands burn them in a crystal ashtray because loose hair, like clipped fingernails, should never be left lying in the open, someone could take them to the humming woman who, on sunny days or for special customers, writes a name once, twice, three times, fourfivesix, seven times in tiny letters, and on top of them, neatly, she wrote seven times, mine, then folded the parchment, sprinkled it with incense, it burned, curling like black tendrils.

"On the night I entered the club she approached me with the quickness, this woman with plaitable hair, and said 'tu danses?' And since I didn't know, then, I said, 'oui, I'd love to dance'; and *aahh* the sea of women parted as she led me across the floor. She placed one hand, here, at the small of my back, and her other hand here (he holds me like that). So what could I do? but hold her, too. Niagara spun *French Kiss* and this woman's hips rolled like thunder beneath my hands, my fleshier hips twirled against hers. *French Kiss* spun as we turned and turned laughing, turned but she didn't step on my toes turning, and I didn't step on hers turning till I was warm, dizzy, and the oils and lanolin of an October evening moistened her forehead, tickled her neck.

"Then.

"The music slowed.

"She drew me near.

"I put my head on her shoulder to stop the room from spinning, she drew me near. Opened her mouth. Her lips were red. Trembling. Her lips were thick, red ... swollen welts covered my body the nights I was one, two *(I said tie your shoe!)* belt buckle at three years old. At four *(shut that damn door when I'm in here alone!)* and at five years old lullabies and salve closed the wounds: Now I lay me down to sleep/I pray the Lord my soul to keep/if I holler let me go *'let him go'* ... eenie, meanie, miney ... nooooo! At six years old, willow switches; sticks leave traces at seven. *(Keep your eyes straight ...)* at eight, and at nine years old (*... keep your legs closed!).* Oh God, when I was ten, when I was eleven; god damn the pain at twelve because warm blood dripped down my leg staining my pants while I was outside playing with the nasty boys: I like coffee, I like tea. I like a white boy he likes me but jump back white boy ... Jump back, I said at thirteen, grabbing a butcher knife. Jump back, not again, no never never again, and this woman? This woman who taught me to *(do what I tell you)* honor thy mother *(honor your mother)* and crave pain? Her lips were red, too. Red as those of the first woman who asked me to dance, warm red as the blood that cried on my lobe where he bit me.

"But now we're poised on the ledge of night. Find your way back, and I'll go to the impasse of gaiety. Go on, go back because tonight he's not walking along the bridges near the Beaux Arts, tonight he's not peering at infant shadows in store windows. Go on, go back because today there was a blue letter written in green ink; and tonight he waits for me."

"Damn it, Kyle, let him go!"

"Let him go? I would if I could but when I arrive the shutters are locked and he's slipped a cassette into the recorder, the equalizer switches are broken. The song is the same, forever the same, and always this music compels me."

Dies irae illa solvet, saeclun in favilla . . .

"He weaves his fingers through my hair to the roots, massages my scalp, kneads my temples unleashing endorphins which hopscotch tension like elves. There's terrible longing in the harmony of men as the women sing, *quantus tremor est futurus* and he looks at my body as if this was the night he first saw that my left breast is higher and wider than my right."

Quando judex est venturus.

"He runs a finger along the trail obsession has zagged across my stomach. *Dies irae.* and the trumpets attack. But what he wants most is to watch my face and I know the contortions it makes when the pains twist inside me anger pounds at the door to my heart till I'll die if he does, and if he doesn't . . . So I squeeze my eyes tight as the legs of virgins, open them just as quickly, and look at the dare in his if he's on top, repressed rage and strangled impulses mirror mine if he's on top, I lick his lashes if he's on top, a tiny gold cross caresses my face; but usually sometimes *always* it's me on top riding the wind as he calls my name. 'Kyle.'

"But his voice . . . I'm far far away.

"I hear another voice, too. *'Don't play in the rain, Kyle, don't*

*run in the summer or you'll perspire and your hair will revert
and I've paid too much money. Do you hear me, Kyle?'*

"Yes, god damn it, I hear you, yes! I'll hear you forever, so . . .

" . . . I . . .

" . . . sweat; and his breath makes me tingle, scream, fuck me, I
shiver when the violins quicken. 'Oh God, love me.' But his voice
. . . far far away . . . "

"Kyle," he calls out. "Wait!"

"So . . .

" . . . I . . .

" . . . wait for blue letters, green ink. But when he calls me,
'Kyle, I love you,' he says when the gold cross caresses my face and
the men sing, 'Kyle, I do not love you,' he says, and the women
echo, 'I will continue to love you in the way that is mine, and that
way, forever, in the still of night.'

"I

" . . . can't . . .

" . . . stop as obsession swims along the faded design in the carpet. Can't stop as obsession spins in the corners of the ceiling,
obsession wobbling on a broken steel leg. No, I . . .

" . . . can't . . .

" . . . stop, come with me to the ledge of night. Come with me
and we won't stop, we won't stop.

"But he can't come in the still of night, he can't come."

"Let him go!"

"I would if I could; he can't come as the neighbors wait in silent
anticipation, he can't come as Jesus falls from the wall, weeping.

"Kyle, let me go," he says simply. "Simply love me."

"He can't come but rides the red tide through boiling seas, the
seas are boiling, the devil is waiting, and it's the rock that cries out

how great a quaking shall there be, when from their graves all men shall rise, to answer to their judge's charge.

"And oh God, if he would only plunge into this luxurious impasse, if he would just come to the anonymous existence of gaiety?

"And what we make, is not love.

"What *we* make, is not love.

"But even fallen angels dance on the head of a pin."

TINA McELROY
ANSA

TINA McELROY ANSA was born in Macon, Georgia, in 1949. She graduated from Spelman College in 1971, where she returned as writer-in-residence. McElroy Ansa's first novel, *Baby of the Family*, was published in 1989 by Harcourt Brace Jovanovich. Her personal essays and short stories have appeared in anthologies including *Breaking Ice*, edited by Terry McMillan and published in 1990 by Viking Press, as well as *Wild Women Don't Wear No Blues: Black Women Writers on Love, Men, and Sex*, edited by Marita Golden and published in 1993 by Doubleday.

McElroy Ansa has also taught journalism and creative writing courses at Clark College and Brunswick College.

Ugly Ways, McElroy Ansa's most recent novel, was published in 1993 by Harcourt Brace & Company. She is working on a collection of short stories, *The Mulberry Tales;* the screen adaptation of *Baby of the Family;* and her forthcoming third novel. Ms. McElroy Ansa lives on St. Simon's Island with her husband, Jonée Ansa.

WHEN I WAS LITTLE, the only thing we didn't have to eat as kids was oatmeal. Because my mother hated oatmeal. I asked her as a little girl why we didn't eat oatmeal, because people at my school, on cold mornings, would have a bowl of oatmeal. My mother made an ugly face and said, "I can't stand oatmeal. It multiplies in my mouth." And I recognized how wonderful her use of that word was, because I immediately started feeling this oatmeal multiplying in my mouth.

The oral tradition has always been very important in my family. Black folks have a real facility with words. We like the sound of words in our mouths, we like to tell stories and hear our own voices. The American English language has been spiced by all of our language—listen to the commercials on television, the music on the radio, listen to slang, listen to words that have become part of the lexicon. We come from a tradition where we used to learn poetry as kids—everybody used to learn an Easter poem, or a James Weldon Johnson poem, Langston Hughes, or Gwendolyn Brooks. The oral tradition is a part of our culture as black people, but it is also something we excel at.

I am a southern child, so I grew up knowing I wanted to be a storyteller. The first time I heard a story, before I could even read, I knew that I wanted to tell stories. I come from a family where you turned the TV off when stories were being told on the porch. Storytelling was something you got attention for. At the dinner table, there were five of us kids, my mother and father, and my grandfather lived with us for a while, so you can imagine that everyone was vying for attention. I knew that if I could tell an interesting story, I could hold court. Stories were important in my family because knowledge was important. Not just book knowledge, although my family was a family of readers, but just *knowing* things. Reading was very respected in my home. My mother would always be reading in this big pink chair that she had, and the one thing we could not do was to disturb her when she was sitting in that big pink chair reading a hardback book. We're not talkin' magazines here, no, *hardback* books. And I was the baby of the family, so I was always running around saying, "Gotta love me, gotta love me!" I would think, "What in the world could Mama be doing that was so important that it could keep her from *me*?" When she got up and left the book on the chair, I would pick it up and look through it. There were never any pictures, just words. And I thought, "Oh God, there's magic here."

I don't really remember asking anyone if there was such a thing as a writer. I think probably the written word became important to my generation because our parents were so tied to education, and so sure that education was our way up and our way out. So my interest in writing probably started out in my home with the stories, and then just naturally went on to books. My stories come to me now in all kinds of ways. My first novel, *Baby of the Family*, came to me in parts. It started as a short story about a little black girl in a small southern town who goes up the dusty street to get her hair done at the beauty shop. She goes regularly because she's tender-headed, and her mother and her grandmother can't stand to see her cry so they send her to the beauty shop to get her hair done. So she walks into the shop, and sees this beautiful dark-skinned black woman whom she had never seen there before. When the dark woman opened her mouth to speak, she spoke with an accent because she was from the Sea Islands.

Later on, the dark woman takes the little girl under her wing and teaches her how to be a real woman—how to be nosy, to know things, to ask questions.

When I sent this story out, and got rejection after rejection, I would cry, work some more on it, send it out again, and get another rejection. Finally I realized that it was not a short story. I needed to know who this little girl was, where she lived, what happened when she got home, what her parents were like, where she went to school. As soon as I knew there were things to find out about this little girl, the story just got bigger and bigger. I knew this little girl was special, and I knew I had to write a novel.

When I first tried to think of a way to make this little girl special, I thought of my own childhood. I think that particularly for emerging writers, we go "out there somewhere" for ideas, because we think that's where all the great ones are. We so often forget that the gold is right inside, in your family, in your community, and in your memories. I was born with a caul over my face, a caul or a veil, which is a thin membrane, or a piece of skin, that some babies are born with over their faces, some over their heads, or their whole bodies. Doctors will say that it is part of the sac that the baby is born in, but it is really more than that. And it happens in all cultures—African-American, Native American, Welsh, Caribbean, South American—it transcends all cultures, and it means that the child is special in some way, or connected with the supernatural. These children are supposed to be able to see ghosts, they are supposed to be able to tell the future, they are supposed to be able to read people just on sight, and also they are supposed to be very lucky. In the black community, the caul marks you as a special child. When I was a kid, the whole school knew that I was born with a caul. And when I had the good sense to realize that the little girl in *Baby of the Family* was born with a caul too, I realized how much rich material I had from my own childhood; from reading slave narratives, from hearing stories of my family history—in all of that there was very strong imagery of the caul, and the specialness of it, the ghostliness of it, and the memory of small communities where people played the numbers because of dreams, and planted corn by the moon, made decisions because of feelings they had, that kind of thing.

The child in the novel is born in 1949, so she is born when I was born, on the cusp of a lot of changes—when black people were trying to move into the mainstream and get away from what they considered old-time, superstitious "nigger jokes." When I was writing this novel, I would so often think of how we as black people have been presented in the larger culture, and I would think about ghosts—because when I would see movies from the thirties and forties and there would be a black person on the screen, if ghosts were mentioned, the black person would say, "Oh Lawd, feets don't fail me now!" and their eyes would bug out, and their hair would stand on end—and I started thinking about what a perversion that was to turn the spiritual and supernatural tradition and history of black people into something so grotesque.

My great-grandmother Nellie Lee told us ghost stories, and she was a very wise person. She would tell us stories that included morals about life—if you live a certain way, you're going to die a certain way; if you love your grandmother or your grandfather in life, he or she is not gone when he or she dies. They are always with you. My great-aunt, Elizabeth Lee, who was a real Christian woman, would tell us ghost stories about how to live that certain way my great-grandmother talked about; how to live upright, and reap what you sow. And my grandfather, Frank McElroy, told us ghost stories purely for scare value, he'd have us screaming and running all over the house. So I remember thinking about all the different ways that ghost stories affected and ran black people's lives, and culture, and how the white, mainstream culture had taken that and turned it into a "nigger joke." So what I really wanted to do in making the little girl in the novel born with a caul, and having her see ghosts and all that, was to snatch back our culture; to snatch back the part of our culture that really comes from Africanisms that tell us to respect and make reference to our ancestors, to make a connection between those who are living and those who have passed on. I really wanted to give these beliefs a sense of reverence.

I live on St. Simons Island, one of the sea islands off the coasts of South Carolina and Georgia. It's an island four miles by twelve miles and is very much a small southern town. My husband calls it Black Folk's Plymouth Rock because so much of the slave trade came through Charleston and Savannah, and then after slavery was outlawed, they used a lot of the estuaries and rivers around here to continue to run the slave trade. An interesting thing happened to me when I moved down to St. Simons Island. I am really attracted to older women, and I have a lot of older black women friends. And what I noticed in talking with these women when I first met them is that the people down here are still talking about feelings, and spirits, and dreams, and even ghosts, with a real unself-consciousness. I couldn't get over it. Over the back fence they would talk about these things. And I would think, "God, that's so wonderful, that's how I remember it as a child."

The older women who I met when I was growing up told me so much and really reaquainted me with my history. For the novel, I had done a lot of reading and research in slave narratives and anthropological works about cauls. There is not a great deal about them, but I found some information, and I read about a tea that is made from the caul. Because children born with a caul are special, they need to be protected, and because they are able to see ghosts, that may include evil ghosts as well as good spirits. So you are supposed to give the infant a tea made from the caul with which she was born in order to blind her from seeing evil ghosts, or ghosts that will scare her or be detrimental to her. When I read this, I didn't really get it. But later on, I was talking with this black woman who worked as a maid in the house behind mine. I'm a gardener, so I am in the backyard a lot, and we took to talking over the fence. Her name is Mrs. Gibson, and we would talk about gardening and what have you.

One day she put her hand on her hip and said, "Tell me, what do you do? You livin' in this neighborhood, I never see you go out to work, I know you got a husband, just what do you do?"

So I told her that I was a writer, and that I was writing this novel, and I told her what it was about. She laughed, and told me that she had a daughter who was born with a caul. I asked her if her daughter saw ghosts.

She laughed again, and said, "She see all kinda things." And then she went on and told me that her daughter used to have these violent, terrible nightmares, and that the older she got, the worse the nightmares got. Mrs. Gibson said that it was okay when her daughter was living with her, but then when it was time for her to go to college, she didn't feel right sending her away while she was having those nightmares.

So my heart was beatin' kinda hard now, cause we were talkin' over the back fence about cauls in 1986. I asked Mrs. Gibson what she did for her daughter.

"Well, Tina," she said, "if I recollect correctly, we took her over to Miss Bessie, and Miss Bessie did somethin' for her."

My heart is really beatin' now. And I asked her what she meant when she said Miss Bessie "did somethin' for her"?

"Oh, Miss Bessie wouldn't let us stay in the room," she said, like it wasn't nothin', "but I think she gave her some kinda tea, cause I saved her caul."

Well I'll tell you, my heart was in my throat. I could not believe it. I was standing here talking to a real person whose daughter had been cured of evil spirits with caul tea! I asked her if it worked, and Mrs. Gibson said, "Well sure it worked, my baby went to Morris Brown College and she lives up in Atlanta now. She got a good job too." At that point, the whole novel just fell open for me. In waves.

Something that black people have always been able to do, and something that I aim to do in my writing, is to make the supernatural very natural. I think Toni Morrison does that, but her supernatural isn't so much natural as it is real. I love her craftswomanship, the attention she gives to words, and to images, and to how things sound on the page as well as out loud. Morrison's writing is very African-American to me. And I think that the supernatural really provides strength for black people— and gives a sense of there being something more than just us. Gloria Naylor also does this sort of thing beautifully, particularly in *Mama Day*. She created the most gorgeous Sea Island, so real, and so right.

The one black woman writer who has probably influenced me the most is Zora Neale Hurston. I took a course with Gloria Wade-Gayles when I was at Spelman College, and she actually introduced me to Zora Neale Hurston. I had never heard of Zora Neale Hurston, and at the time, *Their Eyes Were Watching God* was just being reprinted, sort of just being rediscovered. I grew up in a mid-size Georgia town, and my father owned juke joints and liquor stores, so I knew all kinds of people; people who worked in different kinds of mills, or at the paper plant, prostitutes, pickpockets. My parents gave me a real strong sense that people were people no matter what, that there were no classes of people, especially since we made our living on people drinking our liquor.

What struck me about Zora Neale Hurston is that she really captured everyday, common, working-class people—people who were makin' turpentine, people who picked beans for a living, and then gave them such a wonderful, strong inner life. And I remembered those same people from my father's place—that they were winos, and garbage men, that's what they did, but that they also had love affairs and arguments and fights and raised children and never learned to swim and had questions and souls—I had never seen that on the page until I read Zora Neale Hurston. And what Hurston also did in her work was to give a strong sense of blackness. She *loved* black people. I'm talking about a woman who stood on 125th Street in Harlem and measured people's heads to prove that black people's heads were not smaller than white people's heads. You know what I'm saying? She loved black people, she knew us inside and out, and saw us in all of our different ways of being, and was not afraid to put that on the page. When I think of Zora Neale Hurston, I sort of put up my shoulders and strut.

My work really is woman-focused. The things that attract me in fiction are "women's things"—gossip, stories, the kitchen, gardening, sitting around the hearth, and most of all, getting inside of things; what does family mean, what does community mean, what does freedom mean to a black woman? My husband says that *Ugly Ways*, my most recent novel, oughta have a scratch-and-sniff label because I talk a lot about yeast infections, gettin' pregnant, havin' sex, eatin' pussy—all that really wonderful womanly stuff. I think all black women in this country are crazy as Betsy Bugs. I know if you crazy, you crazy as one a' them. And we are. Crazy as we can be. We would have to be crazy to achieve as much as we achieve in a society that tells us that we are not women, we are not beautiful, we are not feminine, we are not able to be vulnerable, but are still told to "Get out there and do it now, girl!" And we do! We not only do, we overachieve. Bein' crazy ain't all bad. Bein' crazy's all right.

I think that any marginalized person has to know her whole culture, as well as the mainstream culture. She needs to know how to move back and forth, how to say one thing in this situation, and another in that situation, how to speak differently, to be aware of who to trust and who not to trust. I think that that is true of black culture and has touched our lives not just in how we live and talk and think, but certainly in how we write. I'm very blackfolkcentric. I was raised around people who were neither upper-class, or lower-class, or this or that, they was just black folks, like everybody else.

I write contemporary fiction. It is not my aim to write pop contemporary fiction. I certainly want to tell a story, cause ain't no sense in black people writin' if they don't tell a story. But I do want there to be more. I'm tryin' to write literature here. I'm no prima donna, but if ever I complain about the process of my life and career as a writer, my husband says, "Hey, you could be making your living saying, 'You want fries with that?' " And I am very aware that my writing is a gift, a gift that I share with others.

I want my readers to come to my work with something, and to leave with something. I hope that I am a good enough storyteller so that anyone can read my work and say, "Ooh, that was good, that was funny," but I also want people to be able to dig deeper. I think of my writing as sort of like a casserole or a torte. You know, there's a top level—and if you just get that, that would be fine, but if you bite into the whole thing then there's all kinds of different and delicious levels underneath.

From
UGLY WAYS

Look at them stretched out there on my screened porch smoking cigarettes and drinking my husband's liquor. Even talking about smoking that marijuana like some kind of damn black girl hippies. And me laying up here in Parkinson Funeral Home with this ugly-assed navy-blue dress on. Talking about me like I ain't in my grave yet. Hell, I ain't in my grave yet. It just goes to show you what they gonna be like when I really am buried and gone.

Trifling! Trifling women! After all I did to raise them right. Well, alright. Maybe I didn't do a lot to raise them not after the baby was five or so, but I did raise them. I did see to it that they were raised. And raised right. Even if they did have to half raise themselves.

Taught them how to carry themselves. How to keep that part of themselves that was just for themselves to themselves so nobody could take it and walk on it. Tried my best to make them free. As free as I could teach them to be and still be free myself.

How many times did I tell Emily, my middle girl, to pull up that chin, tie up that chin. Look to the stars, I would tell them. Look to the stars. Don't let the whole town see you walking with your head down, like you got something to be ashamed of.

Lord knows this damn little-assed town did try to make them think that. That they had something to be ashamed of. Me mostly. Umph. It's funny really. The one thing In life that they could always look to with pride, a mother who set an example of being her own woman, was the thing that everyone wanted them to be ashamed of.

Well, one thing I can say for them, I don't think they were ever ashamed of me, or embarrassed by me. Never once.

It sure is nice and quiet in here. The Parkinsons always did run a nice establishment. I had forgotten how lovely this old building is. Nice and quiet. Just the way the house used to be at night when I liked it best. Course, 'cause I got my beauty sleep much of the day, I could enjoy the night the way most people couldn't.

In the summer, it was too hot during the day to even think about stirring before four or five o'clock in the afternoon. By the time it got dark, I would have had a good long bath and taken care of myself, hair and stuff. And I would have gotten myself something to eat and looked at a little television. The girls or Ernest would have come home by dark and done whatever I needed doing. And I would have had a little company if I felt like it.

Usually, there would be enough time for a little nap in the evening before I went out to do my gardening. That way I'd be nice and refreshed for my work. What with taking my own time and stopping to rest and admire my work and coming into the house for coffee and to eat something, before you know it, there'd be streaks of color in the sky. And I'd come in and look at movies on videocassettes or early-morning television. Then, lay back down before the girls get up for school.

And in the winter, it was too depressing getting up earlier than afternoon. Seeing the sunlight outside and knowing it wouldn't even be strong enough to warm you if you was to walk out in it. Then, before you know it, the day would start to fade and it would be nighttime. But that didn't do any good because it would be too cold to do any gardening.

But then, in the summertime, it would take so long to get

dark enough for me to go outside and get my work done. Oh, well, like the old folks say, "If it ain't one thing, it's three."

I don't seem to be able to feel the daylight on my skin in here the way I used to, but I am adaptable. Shore am gonna miss my plants, though, my flowers the most, I think. I just planted vegetables that made pretty plants. Collards as big as a small child line the walk to the back door. There's a tangle of mint and lavender by a old painted swing, that has mixed and mated so much that their flowers are variegated shades of purple and lavender and it makes your mouth water to brush by it. My patches of old elephant ears were so big and velvety, almost khaki, they held two and three cups of water when it rained.

In the full burst of spring and early summer, the place was a paradise.

Besides my separate rose garden, I had bushes scattered all through the garden. Delicate ones, high showy ones, trailing, climbing, grown in hedges and bushes and over trellises. Tea to cabbage.

I did so love to dig in the dirt. I was just a born gardener. I could taste the soil and tell whether it was acid or alkaline. When I woke up with dirt under my fingernails, it was some of the happiest moments for me.

My garden is a beautiful thing. This time of year I have as many flowers growing almost as in May. Still got begonias and butterfly weed and cannas blooming along with dahlia, big wide dahlias, and delphiniums and Stokes' asters and chrysanthemums. None of the herbs seem to know it's close to winter yet and with some kind of herb planted at every crossway, turn, or corner of the garden, it's a pleasure just to walk through and brush by 'em.

I guess my garden is the thing I'm most proud of.

Other than seeing my girls do so well, of course.

I also taught them how to be ladies. How to do the things that women need to know how to do in this world. How to sew and clean and take care of a house. Make a beautiful centerpiece out of whatever was growing in the nearest yard or field. Even as a little thing, the baby Annie Ruth could step outdoors and come back in with an armful of fall leaves and branches and make a right nice arrangement. I taught 'em that.

They took care of that house a whole lot better than I ever did or ever wanted to. And when things needed taking care of personally, Betty could handle those white bastards down at the gas company or those hinkty folks at Davison's Department Store as well as lots of grown women. Finally even told that old cracker who used to sit in the lobby entrance from store opening to closing to kiss her black ass when she called her names once too often I was proud of her for that. I probably told her so.

I even taught them to take care of themselves. Many's the time I'd make sure they bought Ivory liquid or Palmolive liquid so when Emily washed dishes she didn't ruin those pretty hands of hers. She does have the prettiest hands. And it was me, nobody else, who taught those three girls how to take care of what they've been given.

How many girls their age know so much about moisturizing their skin as they do? I never let 'em use soap on their faces and made sure there was always some Pond's cold cream in the house. How many other mothers can say the same?

I never was one for lying. At least, I never was after things changed, so I'd tell them right out what their best attributes were and what failings they didn't even need to waste their time on trying to improve.

I didn't coddle 'em and cuddle 'em to death the way some

mothers do. I pushed 'em out there to find out what they was best in. That's how you learn things, by getting on out there and living. They found their strengths by the best way anybody could: by living them.

From the looks of this here dress they bought to bury me in—went out to the mall and bought it out at Rubinstein's, too, know they paid good money for it, the price tag is probably around here somewhere—you can tell they holds a grudge for something though. What in God's name would possess them to go out and spend good money on this navy-blue monstrosity—and they know navy blue is not my color, they know how pretty I look in pastels—when I had all those beautiful bed jackets at home. Hell, some of my old stuff might be a bit outdated, since I ain't had any need for street clothes in a number of years, but even it look better than this shit. They ought to be ashamed. Knowing how those girls love beautiful clothes, I can't believe they weren't trying to say something by picking this thing for me to lie in for all eternity. Them girls got ugly ways about 'em sometimes.

Well, at least it ain't cheap. I never could wear cheap clothes. You know, some people can wear cheap clothes and look right nice in 'em. I never could. If I ever put on anything cheap, it would stand away from my body like paper-doll clothes and just scream, "Cheap! Cheap! Cheap!" My girls couldn't either, wear anything cheap. When they was teenagers, they'd try to imitate they little friends and go down to Lerner's or one of them shops and get some outfit or other. It would be cute in the bag, but as soon as they put it on, it would start screaming, "Cheap! Cheap! Cheap!" and they'd have to give it to one of their cheap-clothes-wearing friends.

Knowing Annie Ruth, she gonna go through my bed jackets and personal things before the funeral to see what she can take back to that Los Angeles, maybe my pink satin quilted bed jacket, to wear with some tight jeans or expensive evening dress.

I can hear her now. "Oh, yes, this was my Mudear's. I just had to have something of hers." Little witch.

God, them girls got ugly ways about 'em sometimes. They must get them from their father's people.

You would think them girls were mad at me for something.

Just like them to be mad at me for something I don't even know. Just like with the damn telephone. They knew good and damn well that I didn't answer the phone unless I felt like it. Never did anything else but that in their memory. But wouldn't they get pissed off with me when they came home from school or one of those little piece of jobs they messed around with and I was nice enough to tell them that the phone had been ringing off the hook all day.

"Hope wasn't nobody expecting no calls," I'd tell them, nice like, too. Then, they would get fighting mad. Well, not really "fighting" mad because then they'd be mad enough to fight they ma and don't none of us play that. I guess I got that to be thankful for, too.

Just the other day I was looking at some talk show, coulda been Ophrah, that was talking about these children. Call them Fragile X. They all looked a certain way, long faces and big ears, and they all had the tendency to fight their mothers. I know it wasn't funny, but I had to laugh. Of course, Ernest didn't see the humor of it when I shared it with him later that night. But he's just about lost all his sense of humor over the years.

I have always tried very hard not to judge my girls too harshly. For one thing, everybody ain't me. I learned that years ago.

For another, they were too young to remember how it was

before. To remember it and appreciate how much better things were after that cold, no-heat-and-no-lights-in-that-freezing-assed-house day when I was able to be what I am. A woman in my own shoes. And they don't hardly remember their daddy any other way than his meek, quiety self he is now.

I guess you can't completely blame the girls because they don't know what their Mudear has done for them. Practically all their lives—to show them a good example.

Wait a minute! What did she just say? "Mudear, now, she the kinda 'ho . . ." What the hell kind of thing is that to say about me, their own Mudear. Have they lost their minds or did they actually find some of that marijuana they wanted?

They ought to know that dope make you crazy!

LORENE CARY

LORENE CARY graduated from St. Paul's School in 1974 and received a B.A. and M.A. from the University of Pennsylvania in 1978. After graduate study at the University of Sussex in England, she worked as a writer for *Time* magazine, and as an associate editor at *TV Guide*. Cary has taught and served on the board of trustees of St. Paul's School. *Black Ice,* Ms. Cary's autobiography, published in 1991 by Knopf, received critical acclaim and has been compared to the autobiographical works of Maya Angelou and Richard Wright. *Black Ice* moves with quickness and singular grace through the adolescent life of a black girlchild. Ms. Cary continues to write and live with her husband, R. C. Smith, and their daughters Laura and Zoë.

MY SENSE OF SELF is layered. It comes from the people I grew up around, mostly women, and many other things. I have been trying to think about the things that I give of myself publicly versus those things that I keep for myself privately. It has been important for me to find a way to combine the two. I want to find a way to have public conversations and discussions about who I am; to find somewhere in between the sort of politician's "striking a pose," which I was taught to think of as male, and the personal, private family life. There ought to be something in between so that we can talk about things that are most important to us. I think that has a lot to do with my sense of self as a writer. Also, finding a way to say things has been important.

I remember thinking while I was writing *Black Ice* about all the ways in which people around me were expressing some passion or power, and the ways in which they were mute. All of this comes in like a kaleidoscope, from my grandmother singing in the choir, to gang warring in the streets and my fear of that. All of these things have everything to do with my being a writer.

I did journalism for years, and part of the reason I did journalism was because I couldn't give myself permission to do any other kind of writing. I was raised in a home and a community where the idea was—you get a job. So I allowed myself to write as long as it provided me with a salary. It took a lot to go from journalism to writing what I wanted to write. The positive side of it was that I knew, and still know, that I needed the discipline as a writer that journalism provided. I was always very suspicious of that sort of— "your thighs are like ripe mangos" stuff, that self-indulgent poetry and fiction. I know that I can be self-indulgent and unable to be self-critical, or too critical, which can be crippling for writers. The discipline of journalism was very good for me.

Journalism was also important for me because I wanted to do something that required me to listen. As for *Black Ice*, I did it for practical reasons, which have dominated my life, like most people: I needed to make a living. My eldest daughter was a toddler. The autobiography was something I could do at home. I'm not thinking about autobiography anymore though. That's enough looking into my own belly button for now.

I love the autobiography as a medium; it goes back the furthest. It is a form that can do protest and art, and it is also a very practical form. I know I did the autobiography because of what Henry Louis Gates, Jr., talks about in his book *Bearing Witness*. He says, "The ultimate form of protest . . . was to register in print the existence of a 'black self' that had transcended the limitations and restrictions that racism had placed on the personal development of the black individual." Autobiography can be self-celebrating but not necessarily self-centered.

As a medium, the autobiography stops time; writers say, "I've walked this journey, come and walk this journey with me," which is what I love. Whether it is black or white, the voice says, "Come around here. Now, am I crazy? Or do you see this too?" That's what I wanted to do with *Black Ice*. The autobiography is also about being straightforward and honest. I thought about trying to fictionalize *Black Ice*, and then I thought, "Come on, guess what, this woman who went to St. Paul's School in the seventies is writing a novel about a woman going to this place called St. Jude in the seventies." That's bullshit. Be straight up; write nonfiction and use discipline.

In some ways I feel like I'm still trying to live up to the words that I have put out there. A lot of what writing has allowed me to do is to override the "no talk" voices. That doesn't mean that they are quiet; it means that I have continued on a day-to-day basis to find an override for the voices that tell me not to take risks. As a mother, and a wife, there is a voice that would tell me not to be so out there. But that's a lot of what being a writer is—trying to override those voices and getting out there further than you normally would.

I think it has to do with expression, and what voices allow you to express and what voices don't. Being mother, wife, daughter even, has to do with other people and their needs. Writing is done not to nurture or to comfort but to express intellectual, emotional, artistic, political, and spiritual passion. So many people have been given no craft, no skills, no avenues, and then America asks them: "Well why haven't you expressed yourself?" Find your passion. It is always turned in on black people too, and that is one of the biggest personal dramas that have political ramifications. That is in autobiography too; what is it in the self that has importance for the group? It's that turning in of passion, that damming up of power. We are stigmatized and restricted by class, race, and so we get this damming up of power.

It took me a long time to begin to transcend those restrictions. There is an awful lot in schools that pulls you that way, and an awful lot that pulls you the other way. I mean, I've got about two hundred pages or so that I ended up cutting out of *Black Ice* that had a lot to do with what I experienced in school, where the power was dammed up.

I went back to St. Paul's School as an adult partly for the students, partly for me, and partly for the young person I was when I was there. I did it to go back and re-meet the school. It was a way of walking through my adolescence again. I also wanted to learn more. When I was a student at St. Paul's, and was on the student council, I learned a lot about the institution. So when I went back, first as a teacher, and then on the board of trustees, I learned that I wanted to learn more about the institution, and find out how it really works. And I wanted to learn how to be a better advocate for things that I believe in.

It is important to take the information I learned when I was a student there and broadcast it, to tell people like myself that they can go to a school where there are ten or twelve students in a classroom, where they can get personal attention. It is particularly important because we've gotten so used to negative images being put into our homes—from the television, for instance—that we forget to demand. Knowing that you are able to demand is a very important function. And it is also important to have more adult advocates who are not white males. As adult advocates we need to just walk through where the kids are still learning and show them that they have someone behind them. When kids don't get what they need, that doesn't feel good to me. I don't like that. And so many of our children get so little. Their lack is an integral element of how America works. They're being educated *not to compete.*

If black people manage to escape from having their life really wrecked by poverty, and I mean poverty wrecks and destroys—marriages, hopes, health and health habits—many who escape tragedy experience enormous guilt. A lot of black students who graduated from St. Paul's don't even think about going back, either because they are working hard enough to keep their lives together, or they don't want to be too close to that institution because they gotta come back and be a homeboy.

Everything in society tells us that if we don't come back and be a homeboy, then we are a sellout. Black people are given very few models in between these two choices, very few models that show us how to live as a culturally aware, intellectually curious African-American person. It is very debilitating. It's also vintage American. America has a strong anti-intellectual strain throughout our history.

Another thing that is real important when you are acting as a role model for the kids is to say, "This is not *the* model, sweetie, but it's one." And of course it is a risk, because it is very possible for the kids to say, "Well we don't like that model, show us another one." But I have to at least give them a model, and I can't give it to them unless I take the risk and put it out there. Then they can either take it or leave it—align themselves with it, or realize they don't want to align themselves with it.

I have been encouraged to demand for myself by many black women writers. Ida B. Wells, Zora Neale Hurston, Sonia Sanchez, Gwendolyn Brooks, Maya Angelou, Toni Morrison, Angela Davis, Kristin Hunter, Bell Hooks, Mary Berry. Individually they have each provided a very strong support system for me and what I do as a writer, and as a conscious African-American woman. The fact of us all together, as a culture of black women writers, is very important. What that means to me is the support of a wonderful spectrum of women who are each different, and that we are many. It was enormously important for me to be taught by Sonia Sanchez and Kristin Hunter while I was in college—to get right up there and touch them, and to see the possibility of black women *doing*. I remember, also while I was in college, interviewing Gwendolyn Brooks. She said that she had written all this stuff and had received all of these prizes, but that she hadn't yet written poetry that could be read in bars. And that is also what inspires me about Ida B. Wells: she went out there into the real world, an ugly, murderous world, and wrote about real people's lives. I respect that enormously. Wells dug up the facts and kept writing. People bombed her office, and she kept writing. Gwendolyn Brooks's writing is unabashed, very womanly, brilliant, and I love the clarity of her language—so clear, so intellectual.

Toni Morrison is so powerful and strong. You go into Morrison's world and the book really says, "Now lie back and let me do this." Jesus I love that. I probably feel the closest to Maya Angelou, closest in my soul. It has to do with the spiritual largeness and generosity of her writing. Angelou's writing has splashes of light like sunshine. It is the amazing spiritual generosity that seems to make all of her writing luminous. I like that her writing can be read by so many people and reaches out to everyone.

I want the people I write about to read what I am writing. I have written about a lot of different types of people, but I try not to write *for* anyone but myself. I find it distracting to write with an audience in mind. Usually I don't write *to* anyone. I'm busy trying to get the words closer to the movie—the movie going in my head. When I do picture an audience, I guess I write to me, sitting in my favorite chair.

I get about writing like a dancer gets about her body. There is the making of one's self into an object, a certain objectifying that happens, or making oneself the subject. One thing is that you have to get far enough away from yourself to be able to write. When I was writing *Black Ice*, I would refeel things, and that was very disconcerting to me. I had to learn to accept sinking into a feeling that I had already felt. And I was afraid of never being able to get out.

I write to save my sanity, but when I *really* write, I go deep. Sometimes I feel like I have gone too deep. And that is scary. I am still trying to work out the generosity of spirit in my own writing, which means my connection to other human beings, my responsibility to give and receive love . . . walking through with grace.

The boys began their vigil in mid-November, hoping and praying for black ice, writing home about it.

The phenomenon they looked for is a clear, glittering ice that forms when it gets cold enough before the first snow to freeze the dark waters of the lakes. The surface acts like a prism to break winter sun into a brilliant spectrum of browns. Below, in the depths, frozen flora pose. Black ice is the smoothest naturally occurring ice there is, as if nature were condescending to art.

I went as far as the safety barrier, but not beyond. Tiny air pockets in the ice crackled under my boots. At the barrier I sat down on the ice, waiting for the cold dark to blow through and cleanse me. I wanted peace and clarity. I tried to think of Ricky, but other thoughts bubbled up. In a day we'd be boarding the buses, then the seven-hour train ride. Then I'd arrive at Philadelphia's 30th Street Station, that welcoming palace with the bronze angel with two-story wings holding the railroad's World War II dead in the form of a limp young man. Then home again to Yeadon, and the visits to my grandparents in New Jersey, and my family on Addison Street.

The stillness did not quiet me; I disturbed it. The woods quickened around me as surely as dolls and statues and trees had come alive in the dark when I was a child. Cold as I was, dark ice chilling me from below as the air seeped into my clothes, my mind conjured up the memory of two hot rooms in West Philadelphia that always smelled of liniment and sometimes smelled of gin. I began to tell myself Pap's old stories. They began in the black night, too.

"Can you imagine how black? With not a light anywhere. So black and dark that women were sure to be home by nightfall, because they didn't know what could be out there. And men, too. *Big* men rushed to get in out of the dark and in their homes—where I should have been, but I had stayed and stayed and stayed. . . .

"But here, in this right hand, I carried a heavy stick, just in case. Cane grows up high, so I peered and peered trying to see, but there's nothing to see in the narrow rows, in the dark, so I listened. I first knew it was there; I knew it; and then I heard it as a rustle." He passed his fingers over the sheet and rubbed his dry feet together like the wings of a cricket. "Just a tiny rustle.

"And I stopped and turned in the darkness to face it. Then I saw it in the moonlight, crouched down low—a white dog, white-white, and I heard the growl in its throat. I felt the sweat in the small of my back. It moved toward me. I took that stick and threw! Hard as I could, I threw it."

He heaved into the air, shaking the bed down to its squeaky springs. When the bed was still, he growled out, with a voice held over from his once broader and younger chest:

"And it screamed! It screamed like a woman, and the moment it screamed, I felt the pain, felt it as if that cudgel had come back and struck me there, on my shoulder." Pap guided my hand over a knot of bone on his shoulder, like a fossil embedded in stone. "That was there the next morning when I woke up, and it's been there ever since."

I rubbed the knot each time to see if it had disappeared, or if the love in my hand might dissolve it.

" 'Poor Henry felt his blood run cold/At what before him stood—' "

" 'Yet like a man he did resolve,' " I answered him, " 'to do the best he could.' "

Pap nodded his approval at my recitation. Then he continued: "I learned," he said, "that some things *thrive* in the dark. One man, Horace, I think his name was, Horace and his wife were getting ready for bed, when a knock came on the door. The door was already shut for the night, and they had, like we all had, a heavy piece of wood that went across to lock it. So Horace called through the door, who was it? And a pitiful voice answered, the voice of a woman who had gotten caught out late and wondered if there was a man in the house to walk her home, just up the road, but she was sooooo frightened. So Horace told her to wait there, and he started to pull on his pants. And then, he was just lifting the bolt off the door, and his wife, it was, said to him, 'Horace, you better take your gun.'

"And then they heard it screech: 'Hah-haaaaaah!' the thing outside the door screamed. 'Your wife saved you!'

"Your wife saved you." He repeated the sentence again in a wee, small voice and laughed to himself.

We never said exactly what it was that was outside the door, but I had no doubt that it was a witch, some vengeful, rapacious spirit. I imagined that the spirits were always women, like the one who slipped out of her skin at night and flew around in the darkness. She left her skin draped over a chair by the window, as easily as others leave their lingerie. When her husband realized what was happening, he went to an old woman in the village and asked how he could keep his wife home with him, where she belonged. The old woman told him to pretend to be asleep that night and wait until his wife was gone. Then he was to take salt and rub it on the inside of her skin. So he did. Just before the following dawn, when the sky began to lighten a little, but the moon still shone white and silver through the window, the husband heard the rustling and then a shriek of pain as the wife tried to slip back in. "Skin, skin," she screamed, "ya na know me?"

I knew the stories so well that I daydreamed sometimes when he told them. I fell into a reverie in which I escaped from the city into a green wood, carrying with me my younger cousin and sister. It would be cold and clear in my fantasy, and the children would have to walk hard to keep up. I'd carry them toward the end, one in the front, the other on my back, until we reached a cave I knew, where we'd shelter from the cold. I'd build a fire to warm us, and keep us there, safe and quiet and gentle. I'd never beat them, and we'd grow up together, simple and strong.

At other times, I'd remember Grammom and her soft, salty food: The *c'coo* she made, a tomato-base fish stew, cooked so long that you could crunch the bones, poured over a green porridge of cornmeal and okra. Her kitchen had felt safe like my cave, safe from the women who now ran the family.

Now that Grammom was dead, Pap seemed to have lost his link to the women downstairs. He was Man to them, the only steadfast, ever-present man in their lives, as much symbol as flesh. He fixed things still, blind as he was, feeling the rotten wood where a screw no longer caught and fingering through an old tool box for a longer screw, the proper screwdriver and putty. But the family had grown out of his stories. Their womanhood seemed to be a taking off from the world of men below: as surely as they worked and worried to get a man and then build a home and a bed in it with him, so too did they seem eager to fly away. I had no doubt that if they could have, my mother and her sisters and my grandmother would have left their skins draped like pantyhose over their unsatisfactory furniture and floated up above us all: the men who never failed to oppress them; the children who'd ruined their beautiful bodies; and the boxy little houses fit to bursting with the leftover smells of their cooking and the smoke from their cigarettes, curling up and hanging just above our heads like ambition.

Pap withdrew from their magic womanhood, even as he praised it. Marrying them off, he said, was like throwing "pearls before swine." We said it to each other as we looked at the yellowing newspaper clippings of my twin aunts at twenty, caught by an admiring photographer at some social function or another, in identical broad-brimmed hats and fur-trimmed jackets.

If they allowed him to withdraw, however, and to ossify into a family icon, certainly he himself had taught them how and why: "There's a man whose daughter is standing at the top of some steps," he began, "and the child's name is Izzy. Now the father told the girl to jump down the steps, jump down to where he was. 'Jump, Izzy, jump,' he said. 'Papa's got you. Papa'll catch you.'

"But she's scared. 'I'll fall, Papa,' she says.

"But he answers her, his voice so gentle, so strong: 'Papa wouldn't let you fall. Don't be afraid. Come on, now, jump, Izzy, jump.'

"Finally the child gathers up her courage and jumps. She leaps toward her daddy's arms—and her father, he steps aside. The child falls, of course. She falls down on that hard ground, and it hurts. She's scraped herself, and it hurts. Her daddy helps her up and dries her tears, and she cries to him and cries and asks him, 'Papa, why didn't you catch me, Papa? Why did you let me fall? You said to jump, Papa, and I jumped.'

"And he says to her, 'Listen to me, Izzy, and listen carefully. 'Learn this this once and never forget: Trust no man.' "

We learned the lesson and whispered it into each other's ears like poison. "Jump, Izzy, jump," we said when one of us fell short, and then we laughed the grim, hysterical laughter of caretakers whom no one took care of.

I remembered Izzy and fashioned for myself the perfect pose. That was it. That was what I'd been trying to remember these months at St. Paul's School, the pose: I would be well-mannered, big-hearted, defiant, and, because a pose cannot resist great intimacy, at the center of all my posing, I would remain alone. I would trust no man.

I got up from where I sat, walked a little farther out onto the ice, and then circled round the pond and made my way to the bank. I was warm with exertion and reverie. Comforted by the old, familiar fears, I could go back again to face the new ones.

It did not occur to me that the ice I had been sitting on might not be the black ice I'd heard about. It wasn't. Black ice is an act of nature as elusive as grace, and far more rare. I did not learn about either until much later.

PEARL CLEAGE

PEARL CLEAGE is an Atlanta-based writer. Author of the best-selling book *Mad at Miles: A Blackwoman's Guide to Truth*, published by The Cleage Group in 1990, Cleage is the founding editor of *Catalyst* magazine and the artistic director of Just Us Theatre Company. Her plays have been performed at theaters and colleges throughout the country, and her most recent play, *Flyin' West*, was presented at Atlanta's Alliance Theatre Company in 1992.

We Don't Need No Music, Ms. Cleage's first book of poetry, was published in 1972 by Broadside Press, and her first book of short fiction, *The Brass Bed and Other Stories*, was published in 1991 by Third World Press. Ms. Cleage has served as writer-in-residence at Spelman College, where she received her B.A. in 1971, and is currently playwright-in-residence at the Spelman department of theater and drama. Her most recent book of personal essays, *Deals with the Devil*, was published by Ballantine books in 1993.

THERE WERE BOOKS all over the place in my house when I was growing up. I came from a family of people who were writing. I'm the first professional writer in my family, but there were always a lot of books and a lot of talk about writers and writing. And a lot of respect for writers. So writing to me was a *real* occupation, like choosing to be a nurse or a minister, because I knew black people who were writing.

I was a young teenager in the sixties when the Black Arts Movement was in full swing. My father is a minister, and he would have writers come and read at the church when they came through town. I was not only around writers, but I was around writers who were not much older than I was. Since my family was very involved politically in the Black Liberation Movement, there was never a question of what to write about. There were so many things going on at that time, so many things that we were doing and thinking and talking about. My writing has really reflected on that experience, and I have always been committed to and deeply rooted in my own life as a black person struggling against oppression in this country.

I grew up in a context of people who were writing to free themselves. I'm real fortunate in the respect that I always knew that I was a writer. I remember being a little child, like maybe two years old, in a crib, leaning over the sides of the crib telling stories to my older sister. When I learned how to read and write, I wrote stories. It was never a question. I always knew that writing was what I was supposed to do, which I think is a real advantage. I knew that I had other skills, and that I would be able to support myself if I couldn't make a living as a writer.

Throughout my life, I have done a lot of other kinds of work—I have been a teacher, and I have worked in public relations and politics. It has never occurred to me that if I couldn't make a living as a writer I would stop writing. I always wanted to be able to make a living at it, but I also knew that the kinds of jobs I could do to support myself were jobs that would not distract me from the writing. The whole idea of making money with my writing actually came much later. I knew that I was going to write, no matter what, so when I started getting paid for it, I was really pleased and amazed.

When I create characters for a play, in the best instances, they are characters who have presented themselves to me. The most recent play I wrote grew out of my readings about Ida B. Wells. While Ida B. Wells was the editor of a newspaper in Memphis, there was a terrible lynching. Wells suggested that black people leave Memphis and go west, taking advantage of the Homestead Act. So seven thousand people left Memphis and went west. That drove me crazy. First of all, that a black woman writer would have that kind of power. Second of all, who were these seven thousand black city people who went to start a new life on the plains of Kansas? When I researched it further, I discovered that a lot of those people were black women, who went without husbands, who went without fathers, who went with their cousins and sisters and other groups of women. Those black women had been kind of amorphous and anonymous to me. Once I got more information about them, they became reality for me.

I'd always rather write it than say it. Whatever *it* is. I enjoy reading my own work sometimes. Reading my writing in front of people is a very different process because I have to be concerned about other things—concerned about drawing people to me, concerned about whether they like it or not after they paid their money to buy my book and see me read. I have to prove to them that they did the right thing by leaving their televisions and coming out to a book reading. *While* I am writing I never think about whether what I am writing will make people like me, or draw people to me. I am much more concerned with whether or not what I am writing pleases me. How does it sound to me? And is it true to the experience I am trying to capture, or to the characters who I have created? When I *do* think of an audience, it is always black women. Always.

Of course I am pleased when anybody likes my work, but I need to write with a specific audience in mind. I know that my experiences as a black woman connect me in a very real way to contemporary African-American women. I'm not sure if I can also connect to black women in Brazil, or black women in Thailand, but I know that my experiences really connect me to my sisters here in America. I'm always trying to get black women to show a nod of recognition—to say, "Yes! That's true!" If black men also have that feeling, if white women have it, or white men, if Native Americans have it—that's wonderful, but my main concern is that I am able to truthfully convey what it is like to be a black woman here in America, at this moment.

The connection I feel with black women, and the connection I feel with black women *writers* is in a way the same connection, because I think of all black women as my sisters. I am connected to black women writers in a more specific way—we all get together and talk about what we are working on, what writing is good, what writing makes us crazy. The black women writers who I don't know personally I still feel very connected to because they are often the ones who give me something to push against—not in a bad way, but just to give me a sense of perspective. They are there to say:

"Don't start thinkin' you're the be-all-end-all, because remember Alice Walker, remember *The Temple of My Familiar*. Don't start thinkin' you've written the most wonderful autobiography, because remember Maya Angelou."

Black women writers make me take my work seriously, make me want to not fall down on the job. All I have to do is think about how hard Toni Cade Bambara has worked, or how hard Toni Morrison is working. I think black women writers have a stronger sense of community than black male writers, who appear to be more fragmented. I don't think John Edgar Wideman and the *guys* talk to one another, or feed off of each other like we do. And that could be a gender question. I think that black *women* just constantly seek one another out because we need to know that we are all writing.

It is necessary for me to know that I am not the only one doing this—I know that Tina McElroy Ansa is up the road, and I know Terry [McMillan] is on tour. We all inspire one another. There is also a strong support in knowing that my sisters before me were writing. I remember reading Zora Neale Hurston's *Their Eyes Were Watching God* and thinking, "My God, *this* is a love story." Nella Larsen, who wrote about being a light-skinned black woman in both her novellas, *Quicksand* and *Passing*, was very influential for me. She was able to write about the experience of "the tragic mulatto" without any sort of preciousness. I think she tried to incorporate different politics around the issue of Passing way before her time.

Maya Angelou's autobiographies are very important for me because she wrote nonjudgmentally about having a full life. It was very liberating to read her work, in the sense that I knew that I would not have to be concerned about censoring any of the stories that *I* needed to tell.

I have been very inspired by one black male writer in particular—Langston Hughes. He was and continues to be the most comforting of all black writers to me. Hughes was able to begin writing because of his connection to black people. He really loved black people. Throughout his life, he continued to be grounded in the black community and was utterly devoted to writing about *real* black folks. I think his work is a wonderful tribute, because anyone can start out wanting to stay grounded in the black community as far as their writing goes—but like any group of people, we can drive one another crazy. The fact that Hughes was able to structure his life as a writer around black life is really important for me. He made it possible to embrace the whole world while still upholding the strength of one's own culture.

I wouldn't even know how to separate being black and being female. And I wouldn't want to. The challenge for me has been to become as conscious and articulate about what it means to be female as I am about what it means to be black. I grew up in a very race-conscious family that articulated to me at every turn what it meant to be black in America.

There was *comfort* around the issue of race. By comfort I mean that I understood I was a member of a group that was oppressed, and that the oppression wasn't a personal thing—I wasn't the only one who lived in a community with problems, I wasn't the only one who had problems with unemployment, I wasn't the only one feeling the impact of oppression. My experience was a group activity, and one group was oppressing another group. The personal, individualistic response to my experience was removed. I never felt as though I wanted to "lift" myself out of my group and be rewarded by white people. I didn't want to leave my community and move to a white community so that I could have a better life. I wanted to focus on what my group could do to improve our situation. Understanding race and racism within my family and everywhere else was and *is* invaluable, because it meant that I didn't have to feel confused and wonder, "Why is this happening?" I knew why.

My family was not necessarily a feminist family, so I didn't have the same grounding in terms of what it meant to be female in a sexist society as I did in terms of what it meant to be black in a racist society. So I took on the feminist issue for myself when I was much older. I was about twenty-five years old when I bumped up against a lot of feminist work and activism. I was very exhilarated by the fact that the feminist movement addressed all kinds of questions that I could answer about race, but not about gender. And I knew I could learn. I read everything I could and talked to people to acquire the same degree of understanding and fluency about what it meant to be a woman as I did about what it meant to be black.

I believe that there are things that we can't articulate and understand in the language that we have. Human beings are not the be-all-end-all of the universe. There are bigger things and greater questions to which we are connected. We are connected to everything that is present in a way that I think has more to do with African culture than it does with the sort of general white American culture. I feel very connected to my ancestors, my personal ancestors, especially black women ancestors who have been here for a long time, struggling, working, and raising their children. I feel a real responsibility to them and a real source of strength from them.

I don't think my generation is the first generation of black women that ever struggled, or that we are the first generation that ever established we had a right to a place in the world. So I feel very connected to Ida B. Wells, Zora Neale Hurston, Anna Julia Cooper, and all of those women who came before. And I don't really think you necessarily have to be a black woman to feel empowered by those women. I think that for white women there would be a strong sense of gender connection. In the same way that if I read Maxine Hong Kingston, I feel empowered by what Chinese-American women have done throughout their struggle. If I read a book by a Native American woman, then I connect to the fact that our struggles as women are very similar, even though they manifest themselves in very culturally specific ways. There are certain things that women as a gender experience. Some of these things are bad things, like sexism, but some of them are wonderful things, like having babies. As women, we can plug into one another's strengths as long as we can get past our own racism.

My mother taught me that preciousness is not acceptable when there is similar struggle around you. She would tell me, "Don't get too full of yourself, you're not the first one to do it, and you're not gonna be the last, so take your place in the line and do the work you are supposed to do." I love the quote from Audre Lorde: "The real challenge in life is to get done the work I came here to do before they nickel and dime me to death."

The important thing is to stay focused on what you are doing, and not get distracted by all of the other things, but to have a strong sense of all of the other things—what they are, what they do, and who they are. We are all connected in some way.

There are experiences that I have had that involve other people in a personal way. I would not write about these experiences, although I would love to, out of respect for the person involved in that experience. Usually I write in a very personal way, and so the most important value for me is to not cannibalize my own life to the degree that I betray the people who are closest to me. It's called personal integrity. I had to give myself permission to write about myself, what I see, and what happens to me. When I realized that there were other black women writers doing

PEARL CLEAGE

the same thing, I felt connected to a sisterhood and not so self-absorbed. It wasn't as though I was saying, "Look at me! Look at me!" I want for people to consider me as a writer who is connected to others.

I am often moved to continue writing by a quote from Alice Walker's *Possessing the Secret of Joy*: "Resistance is the secret of joy." I was really raised to believe that. Walker said it in such a succinct way. For an oppressed person who is not in a rarified world, I know that resistance *is* the secret of joy. I don't know if it is true for someone who is rich and famous. I think that the real happiness, the real joy in your existence, has to come from struggling for your freedom. Because if you are not struggling, you are collaborating with the enemy in your own oppression. Which doesn't mean that you can't also have children, and love people, and drink mimosas with your friends, and giggle over their love affairs. It means that you do all of that in the context of struggle—so that those love affairs are in the context of an ongoing struggle for black men and black women to communicate honestly, so that having a child becomes a process of trying to raise that child to be aware of the world around her.

Being constantly involved in revolution may seem like a dreary life to some people. I don't feel that way. I feel that I am much happier than most people who have straight jobs and are making a lot more money than I make, because they are always trying *not* to be angry, *not* to see the truth, *not* to be a part of everything. Whereas I am always trying to strip away the artifice and tell the truth about everything. I do that in my writing, and I have no fear of what I may find. I am not afraid of what I may discover inside myself. I want to know everything that is in my head, everything that is in my heart. I know that there isn't anything bad in there.

From

DEALS WITH THE DEVIL

Daughters of the Dust

I went to see Julie Dash's film, *Daughters of the Dust*, for the first time on a recent Thursday evening. Now, I had been missing *Daughters of the Dust* screenings for at least a year. I would either be leaving town the day before somebody screened it, or be arriving someplace where it had been screened the day before. It got to be funny as more and more women asked me if I had seen it, and I tried to explain that I almost had, but . . .

"You've got to see it," they would say with great intensity. "You've just got to see it."

Now, I always take recommendations like these seriously. That's the way people told me to read *Disappearing Acts* by Terry McMillan as soon as I could get my hands on it, or to go see Sweet Honey in the Rock next time they came to town, or to be sure and hook up with Johnnetta Cole when she came to town to become president of Spelman College.

These recommendations are always made by other black women, and the tone they reserve for these exchanges is so highly charged with sisterhood advice for survival and better living that I know it is foolhardy to disregard them. Sisterhood is powerful and my mother did not have a fool for a child.

I didn't know quite what to expect since nobody could really tell me what *Daughters of the Dust* was about. "It's beautiful," they would tell me. "It's like a dream." I could feel the skepticism on my face. "It's about us," they would say when I pressed them to be specific. "It's all about us."

I sometimes continued to press them but I knew what they

meant. They meant that somehow Julie Dash had managed to write and direct and produce a film that showed African-American women like we really are, instead of tossing us off as one stereotype or another. They meant we're going to be presented as fully rounded people, with the full complexity we know to be our birthright as human beings and our special legacy as African-American women who have survived. They meant that Sister Julie had done on film what Toni Cade Bambara and Toni Morrison and Alice Walker and Paula Giddings had done in print.

Well, I had seen *Jungle Fever* and *Juice* and *Boyz N the Hood* and *Straight Out of Brooklyn* and enough rap videos to be tired of what *the boys* were telling us we looked like to them. I wanted to see what we looked like to us. As the lights went down, I sent a good vibe to Julie sitting in the crush of people up front in the crowded theater, and another to the lady with the fussy baby sitting too close for comfort, and turned my attention to *Daughters of the Dust*.

But wait a minute. I was immediately confused. *Who was talking? What were they talking about? What was the problem? Who was the little girl? Which ones were the newlyweds? Why was Eli so angry? Had somebody been raped?*

My brain was clicking frantically along at the rhythm of the *real* world—the *material* world—demanding the answers required in first semester journalism classes, but Sister Julie refused to indulge me. She was too busy putting together the amazing images on the screen before me—a woman in a billowing white veil standing in the prow of a small boat that is somehow steadied by her mysterious presence; an ancient woman squatting in the water with all her clothes on; a glass of water placed on a letter beneath the bed; a Muslim man at prayer by the water's edge; a book whose pages are gently rippled by the wind.

But who were these people and what were they talking about? I was confused, frustrated, restless. I wanted a road map, a clearly defined path that would use the same guideposts that I was used to depending on to navigate the shark-infested waters of modern-day, racist, sexist America. My brain was still racing along at urban hyperspeed and I wanted *Daughters* to hurry up and get on board.

That's what I *thought* I wanted, but Sister Julie was having none of it. She had placated and translated for enough money people and distributor people and second-guessing people to decide that when it finally got down to the individual moment in the darkness when each individual somebody has to look at the film and decide for herself if it makes any sense, that she, Julie Dash, was going to do just exactly as she pleased. And I understood all that, but I still *didn't understand/didn't understand/didn't understand.*

But then, just at the moment when I began to doubt the wisdom of my sisters whose urgings had lead me to the theater, a group of beautiful young black girlchildren appeared on the screen. They were playing on white sand at the edge of the blue Atlantic. They were laughing and tossing their braids and shaking their dreadlocks and switching their behinds in a game I remembered from my own girlhood on Detroit's west side: "Jump back, Sally, Sally, Sally, Jump back, Sally, all night long . . ."

Say what? "Here comes another one just like the other one . . . " and they collapsed in giggles as one of their number strutted herself down the middle of the line like she knew exactly how lovely she was, and wasn't it wonderful to be young and black and female and safe and dancing by the ocean?

And all of a sudden I understood. Not at a level that I can articulate in words, here or anywhere. But at the level that is quintessentially black and female, no matter who says what about it. At the level that is so exactly what I am that I don't even discuss it anymore since nobody gets a vote but me.

And my sisters. Because we know what is real and what is nonsense. Because we know we carry the genes of our mothers and our grandmothers and their grandmothers all the way back to where we were free women. Because we have what Martha Graham has called "blood memory" that transcends those things that can be put into words even by someone as passionate about words as I am— and must instead be understood in the marrow of the bones, the rhythm of the heart, the fullness of the womb.

That's the memory and the promise and the comfort and the strength and the courage and the truth of what I saw on the screen in front of me as Julie Dash's amazing film unfolded and I laughed and cried and clapped and hollered and felt stronger and wiser and more at peace because she had shown me the best part of myself right up there in living color and, to quote Sister Ntozake Shange, "I loved her fiercely."

So fiercely that I went back to see it again the next day with Sister Stephanie, and the next day by myself again, and the next weekend with my sisterstudents who stood on the sidewalk outside the theater with me while we shouted secrets at each other until the usher came out to tell us the people in the movie couldn't hear what Sister Julie had put together for them because we were making so much noise. And I wanted to say, *it's all the same dialogue if you just know how to listen!*

And watch. I've seen *Daughters* four times now and I wish I could see it every day, just to remind me that I'm not crazy. Just to remind me of how beautiful we are. Just to help me remember how good it feels to be safe and free and happy enough to play girlchild games by the edge of the sea.

Art historians will tell you that when gallery owner/photographer/critic Alfred Stieglitz first saw the paintings of artist Georgia O'Keeffe he exclaimed, "At last—a woman on paper!"

I know how he felt. Toni Cade Bambara says *Daughters of the Dust* is "the film we've been waiting for all our lives." And she's right, just like always. So if you haven't seen it, go see it. Twice. Take your sister. Or your daughter. Or your mother. Or all of them. Because it's about all of them. All of *us*. And, trust me, we never had it so good.

J. CALIFORNIA
COOPER

J. CALIFORNIA COOPER is the author of four collections of stories published by Doubleday—*Some Soul to Keep, Homemade Love* (winner of the 1989 American Book Award), *A Piece of Mine* (originally published by Alice Walker's Wild Tree's Press and then reissued by Doubleday), and *The Matter Is Life*. She has also written two novels, *Family* and *In Search of Satisfaction*, also published by Doubleday. Cooper has authored seventeen plays, many of which have been produced and performed on the stage as well as on public television, radio, and college campuses. In 1978 she was named Black Playwright of the Year for *Strangers*, which was performed at the San Francisco Palace of Fine Arts. Among her numerous awards are the James Baldwin Writing Award (1988), and the Literary Lion Award from the American Library Association (1988). She is currently working on another collection of short stories, which is due out in 1995. Ms. Cooper lives in a small town in Texas and is the mother of a daughter, Paris Williams.

THE WAY I STARTED OUT using pencil and paper was by making paper dolls. When I turned eighteen, my mother made me stop playing with paper dolls, so I started to write down their stories. Then I began writing plays. I got involved with theater groups, and they put on a couple of my plays. From there the plays started to spread out, and then get produced on TV. I was and am just as surprised and excited and happy as anybody at my success—but I never thought of fame because I never thought that the writing was good. I just knew I liked it. I still don't know if it's good. I'm just very fortunate. I happen to be able to say what I want to say, and people listen. I have a lot of strong beliefs, that's all. And I have a lot of thoughts. All you have to do is see people, and you have a lot of thoughts.

My characters come to me with their own stories. Sometimes I think along *with* the characters—we almost always all know where we are going, we just have to figure out how we're going to get there. It's wonderful when my characters come. It's marvelous! I love them so much! I look for them, and I prepare for them. I don't particularly care for company unless it is business. I would love to have company, but I can't afford to have company, because then I won't have room for my characters. So that means when I'm working—and I am working most of the time—then I am at home, and it is quiet, and my gates are locked because I can't stand drop-ins. I never write away from home, so when I'm through with the writing, then I get to take off for a while and go somewhere.

I don't analyze my work patterns, I just write until it's time for me to do something else. Every morning at about five-thirty is when I do my best thinking. When it gets to about four-thirty in the afternoon, I'm not doing any thinking. I just want to lay down and rest, and get something to eat! It doesn't worry me that my mind may need a break at some times in the day, as long as I am using it, you know, feeding it. My mind likes to get up in the morning, look out at the day coming, get a hot cup of coffee, put the right music on that's gonna suit what I'm trying to do that day, feed my little soul, and then go in to the writing and sit down.

I do what my mind says do. I know my mind likes beauty, so there are all kinds of beautiful things around my house. I know it likes natural things—my carpet is green and my walls are wood, because my mind likes the natural world. My whole life is fixed so that some part of me is pleased no matter where I am—in my house or in my yard or wherever. That's why I can't let everybody in it, because I believe in vibes and things, and some people mess with your stuff.

My writing is an accumulation of information from things I've read, things I've seen and observed. My mother used to tell me: "Any fool can get some fun, you need to get some sense." My love for reading came from her, because her head was always in the books. Since I was a little girl, I have always liked wisdom. As a child, I could sit forever and listen to old people talk about wisdom. And they would tell me about life, so now, I never really have to sit down and wonder what I will do in any circumstances because I almost always know. I know I'm going to stick to the truth, and I know I have limits. And that's all!

The truth that I have and the truth that my characters have are of course different. Usually I have a main character, or maybe two or three, depending upon how smart they are, and that main character is doing what I need to have told in the story, telling my truth. But there will always be other characters offering other truths. If I'm gonna write about life—life is full of everybody—so I'm gonna write about everybody! Most important, no matter what their truths are, the characters have to be real.

I like real things! I don't write to amuse or entertain people. I don't like to sit and make stories up. I don't make stories up. I wait and listen for my characters to tell me their stories. If they make it too easy, then I'll say, "That's too easy, we're not gonna do that." Then they'll come back with something else. And we try it again.

I had this woman approach me at a book signing once, and she said after she had read *The Matter Is Life*: "Your books aren't like they used to be, I don't identify anymore." And I wanted to say to her, to this little black woman, about fifty years old, I wanted to say: "Have you lived everything? I'm not writing for you, I'm writing for people who need to know something that may help them through. I'm not writing for one person." Could she read about the devastation of a prostitute? I don't identify with all of my characters, but they blow my mind. I don't want to have to live everything and to identify. But do I have sense enough to know that each character's story is true? Yes!

I haven't made myself up at all. Whatever comes out on the page, that's how it comes. And I don't ever really feel uncomfortable with what comes out. When I wrote the short story "Vanity" though, that was hard. It wasn't so much hard for me to write as it was hard for me to read. Consequently, I haven't read it but once. I didn't like saying all those things. Vanity herself, the character, was boring to me after a while. People addicted to crack are. If she hadn't been so important for youngsters to see, then I probably never would have written it. I should have said more about what men do with that experience, but the men didn't come. Vanity came. And she loved herself. She had to love herself. To take herself out like that, to remove herself from life the way she did, she had to love herself, because that's all she had. I don't think I'll write that story from the men's view, I think that story is over.

If someone shows up though, and I never know who's coming, then I'll have to sit down with him.

My characters when they come to me are all usually such a pleasure. They really are. I go through pains with them, but when they are happy and they do something right, I'm oh so happy. Writing is a pleasure. I meet so many new people. New friends, new children, you know, they're my babies. And I learn so much! When I wrote about a blind girl in *Feeling for Life*, I used to be surprised I could see when I got up from the typewriter with her! There are so many things about the world I didn't realize until I wrote her story. I had to go from scratch with this poor woman. But we did it together. And it is a marvel. That is why I look in my eyes and say, "I love you! I love you!" Because I do. If I could kiss my eyes I would!

I like a good story. Sometimes I have to tell myself one, but those aren't the ones I write. What I hear when I write is truth and wisdom. I wouldn't be able to hear that if I didn't have my own foundation of truth. Because people lie a lot. Sometimes they lie so much they can't even find the truth. But the real truth is so clear. It is in the Bible. What is good and what is evil? I know because the Bible says: "From good does not come pain; from evil invariably there will come pain." The Bible also says that respect is the foundation for love—you can have no love without it. If you look in your mind and think—"Who did I ever love that I didn't respect?" You won't be able to think of anyone. I can't. And if you can, you know you didn't want to love that person. Love doesn't go without respect.

One thing I do know about the truth is that it is not abstract. Even Einstein's theories were not hard to concentrate on. They made logical sense, because a truth is not difficult to see. I don't believe in the intellectual type of sounding smart, that to me is not necessarily the truth. Because the devil sounds smart. Many con-people sound smart. All kinds of people who lie sound smart. But you don't have to struggle and sweat over the truth. The truth is reasonable.

I think that love is reasonable, but a lot of things that people do and call love isn't. How many happy women are there in the world? How many women are there who are happily married? I think there was even a poll taken recently where they asked women what they wanted in a husband. All these women wrote in and said they wanted him to have good looks, a college degree, a pay equivalent to their own or better, a good car. Not one person said honesty or faithfulness. Nobody said values. It didn't come up. All kinds of people are doing all kinds of things, and it doesn't make them smart. What I am saying is that your value system has to be in order for your love to be right.

In the book that I am writing now, there is a woman who is telling a man about her feelings. She has been through a lot with this man, and it has mostly been misery—mostly she has had wrinkles on her brow instead of smiles around her lips, so she tells this man:

"Listen, I'm gonna have to let you alone"—now these are my words, not hers—"because I didn't know I didn't respect you, but I know it now when I have stopped respecting myself for what you are making me be—I'm jealous, I'm a shrew, I'm a nag, I'm suspicious, I'm sneaking around at night trying to see where you are, and I don't want to be that woman."

And he said, "Yea, but you love me."

And she said back, "I love you, but I don't *want* you."

She called it love, but what was she going to say—"No, my id is connected to my unconscious . . ."? No, she wasn't gonna say that. Not wanting him was a good enough justification for leaving him. What I am saying is that there are too many women and men out there who lie too much to each other.

For example, in Terry McMillan's *Waiting to Exhale*, she described women perfectly because we are still waiting to exhale! There are no answers in holding your breath. When you tell a truth, you can exhale. This woman in the book I'm writing told this man that she wanted him to be honest and faithful and he said, "Well, I'll marry you." She tells him, "I don't want to get married just to get a man, I want to get a husband. I want to love him and I want him to love me." So when you are looking for somebody who you're going to spend your life with, you need to have a strong sense of what you want. Not just someone who stirs your insides! Somebody who is going to stay and be faithful and help you raise your children! Someone who will stand by you when you are ill, somebody who you *want* to stand by you when you are ill. Love is much more than a passing feeling, or an orgasm. Some people are in love and never have orgasms, but let me not go there. People and what they do does not change the truth of love. No matter what you call a rose, it's still a rose, you know what I'm saying?

I love and enjoy being a black woman writer alongside of others out there, but nobody inspires me to write. Really, I was writin' before I could read! I was tellin' stories before I could talk! When I walked into the first black bookstore in Oakland, I was so pleased when I saw all those books by black women writers! I had never seen that. I've always loved books. I graduated from high school, got married and all that, and then didn't write, because I didn't think I could. But for the past ten years or so, my books have been getting published, and people are calling me up, so I've just kind of said, "Well maybe I *can* write."

What I like about myself as a writer is not that I write, or that I am a black woman writer, but that I don't lie. It's difficult to say which black women writers I really like, because I haven't read all the white writers. But I know what I think of some black women writers. Alice Walker really got to the point in *The Color Purple*! She didn't mess around! Gloria Naylor did a wonderful job getting into other people's lives with *Bailey's Cafe*. And that is what I like about writing as a way of life—you are getting into other people's lives. I love Toni Morrison's *The Song of Solomon* and *The Bluest Eye*. I like things that will hit, hit, hit! You know, make me think! Not everybody who writes can write. I'm proud for them, and happy for them, but I think a lot of books are empty, they're not saying a thing. The library is full of empty books. A book is a brain, and there are a lot of empty brains in the world. There are certain places where I keep books. If it's in the bathroom, then it's an okay book. If it's beside my bed, it's a good book.

I think that we as black women writers should be proud of who we are, but not be controlled by what we are. Because before we are black, and before we are woman, we are human. So as writers, we need to write from the human experience. My mother always said: "Listen, you don't have to *find* yourself, all you have to do is *be* yourself." So I have never tried to create any identity for myself. I never had to put my blackness and my womanness together. I have been the victim of prejudice sometimes, enough to know that there is a difference when you are black and a woman. But on the other hand, I am healthy. I am able. I can see, I can hear, I can move, I can walk! I don't really give a damn what somebody thinks of me. And that is why I tell people to love themselves, because you are all you have. I love myself so much sometimes I can't see straight! I kiss my knees, my arms, whatever I can reach! I kiss my hands—I am so glad my hand works when it reaches for a glass of water, turns off the air conditioner, cooks my food, it does everything for me! My heart is beating! I am a miracle! I can't do anything but love me! All I do is run my business, build my world, live in it, let people who can fit in it come in it sometimes, and put them out when they can't, because I like peace, and that's that. I am me. I never think about my identity. I know what I am. Nobody can tell me who or what I am because they don't know.

Sometimes I get lonely, but it is better than being with someone who you don't enjoy. I have friends on different parts of the earth who I can talk to on the phone, and I am sure that I will fall in love again someday. But I don't know. I've been married a few times and that's quite enough. You get to a certain age and you get used to eating when you're hungry, and going to sleep until you're ready to wake up. But being with someone is wonderful, too. I just leave it open, and what life brings, I'll handle it when it gets here.

I don't look at people like most people do, I look at people like God does. God never cared about color, not for one minute, not for thirty-five seconds. He cares about how good you are. So I don't separate people by colors. I am proud of being black, but I don't think of it because it is automatic. When I deal with people who do separate color, in order to let what they say affect me, I would really have to think a lot of them, and I really don't. What are they? Now, if they have the mortgage on my house and they are about to foreclose because of my color, then I will go get a lawyer who is *their* color and fight it! The world is big. My mother used to say: "Anybody you don't have to take home with you, you don't need to worry about." The Bible says not to pay attention to another human being unless they're telling you right, and even if an angel is telling you something, check on it!

The exclamatory nature of my stories is the way I perceive life. My characters don't live in periods, they live in exclamation points! And so do I. You can't tell a story that may be full of fear, devastation and importance, or joy and fascination, and then put a period at the end. That's an exclamation point. And life is full of them. Life is full of laughter too. I love it when I laugh!

Like I said, I don't analyze my writing patterns, but there are a few things I know. If it rains, I'm going to get a story. If my house is clean, and there are no dirty clothes anywhere, somebody's gonna come and tell me a story. If my house is junky, nobody's coming. If the sun is burning outside, I can make something up that I already know, or already wrote, but I can't get a new story. And it is sunny here in Texas! It gets to the point where my mind starts developing a conversation with a new character a day or two before it rains, so that I can say, "It's gettin' ready to rain." Isn't that strange? And why that is, I do not know. That's why I'm trying to move to Seattle, where it rains all the time!

From
THE MATTER IS LIFE

Sometimes he would come to Vanity and sleep only on top of the covers, while she lay beneath them, body smoldering, longing for him to enter her. But he would not get into bed . . . let lone into her, tho she begged.

Jody did not kiss her from the feet up. For the first time she longed to kiss him from the feet up, but was afraid her beauty would not look good from that distance. He kissed her lips . . . when she asked him, or when she seemed to be gettin tired of longing for him, ready to quit her grief. He would not see her for five, six, seven, eight days at a time. Let her suffer.

He made dates with her. Then she would do a lot of cleaning. Herself! Cooking, setting the table, puttin out flowers, all of it. Then, looking out the window, sittin, waitin for him. . . . He did not come. Then . . . she looking into that magic mirror . . . to see what was wrong. She saw lines, wrinkles that were not there. In that mirror, when he did not come, and she could not . . . her beauty faded, faded.

She began to buy him clothes, lay them all out on the bed. If he didn't come . . . she would want to throw them all away, give them away. But, she never did, because she had the good sense to know she really wanted this man and would need something to lure him. She "forced" money on him, which he never asked for, just needed, but he took. He folded away, smiling, hundreds of dollars that disappeared deep into his pockets, never to be seen again.

Valentine's Day. No card. He didn't call.

Birthday. No card first year. Only a card the next year . . . late.

Christmas. The second time. A handkerchief. Not wrapped.
Easter. No card. No eggs. Not even his.

Thanksgiving. Said he had to work, needed the money. She cried, again, for she had cooked a full, good meal . . . for him. She couldn't eat.

All the time, he was having a good time with the money from his other little old ladies and his woman. Yet . . . he really was with nobody in his heart. Nobody at all. Vanity spent so much money on him to ease the worry he said was on his mind, made me sick! I mean, really sick, I got ill.

Vanity asked that man to marry her. Marry her! She wanted a lifetime of all that pain. That's what she was askin for! He said he had never planned to marry. He didn't trust women to be true to him. Now! She tried to convince him of her love and faithfulness. He thought about that, a long, long time. Sometimes, he looked into that golden mirror he had given Vanity. Looking at his own beauty. Thinking of marryin Vanity. Of livin in the dark, cause Vanity kept her house darkened. She thought she looked better that way.

Once or twice, when he had come to Vanity, he had been a little sick. She cared for him better than anyone else he knew. Vanity! Caring for somebody else! In a day or so, he always felt better and left with some money.

When she spoke to him of marriage again, he thought a moment, then asked for the use of the little roomette she had in her yard in the back. She gladly gave it to him, tho she said he could stay in the house with her til he decided. Til HE decided. Her Guardian Angel just stayed quiet and grieved all the time now.

He took the roomette, but did not LIVE in it. He used it a lot. He liked to be alone, he said, so she often just looked out at the little house, glad he was out there, close. She would cook and take him food. Sometimes he didn't let her in, said he would be on in her house, later.

Often, when he did come in later, he would be so shinin and sweet to her. He kissed a lot and spoke much of her beauty. But he didn't make love much. He sure talk to her tho!

"My lord! You are so beautiful! So beautiful to me! How do I deserve you? You could have anyone in the world you want you are so beautiful."

Vanity's answer, always, was, "But I only want you."

She began to pester him about lettin her come visit him in the little house. "What did he do there? Couldn't she be with him? She would be quiet, not bother him. He wouldn't have to make love to her. She wouldn't ask him or touch him." Can you magin a woman sayin that to her man?

She told him one day, "I always look so beautiful to you when you come out of your hideaway. If I was in there with you, and I was quiet, I could look beautiful to you longer. In there."

He said no, and no, and no, no, so many times. Til he looked at her one night, thoughtfully. She was sittin there with little tears in her still lovely eyes, waiting, waiting for any little sign he loved her. I hate to think she was such a fool! but I don't know bout this kinda love!

He answered, touching her cheek, "Soon."

"Soon" came one night when he needed some money and asked for it for the first time. She hesitated, cause she thought that would help him leave. He read her mind, said, "I will let you come with me to my hideaway." She gave him the money. He left. He was back soon this time.

He looked at her another long time. Then sighed, and said, "Give me one half hour, then come."

She did. Her Guardian Angel cried aloud, screamed to her, "Beware!" then wept again.

The little hideaway was darkened. Persian type blankets and carpets covered everything. A small, low table on the floor was draped, covered with little saucers and things. He sat her down beside it, smiled down at her, warily. He then picked up a pipe. A pipe he used for free-basing cocaine.

The Guardian Angel could not come in, but he pounded at the door and screamed for Vanity to hear. She did not hear. She was looking at the man she loved, smiling. Just like a lady.

Jody fixed the pipe. Used a lighter to heat the stem til he reached the rock inside and melted it. Drew the first breath, blew it out. Took another breath, closed his eyes and held it in. Opened his eyes, smiled, and handed the pipe to her. Said, "Do what I do."

His hand reached out, slowly. His beautiful, powerful, strong hand that had held her, stroked her, seemed to love her. He held that hand out to her with the cocaine-rock, crack, in the pipe. She already loved that hand. She remembered only the pleasure it had held for her. Her eyes, lovely tho wrinkled around, misted, than clung to his smiling face.

She took the hand, that then gently removed itself from the pipe, leaving it in her once lovelier hand, then gently raising it to her once lovelier lips. Her eyes held to his own. Just like a lady.

Then? Then . . . she slowly finished lifting the pipe to her lips, closed her eyes with the imprint of his smiling face in them, pursed her lips and drew her first breath from the pipe. The magic pipe. She opened her eyes, the smoke wafting slowly through her body, inundating her brain, while looking at this gorgeous man. Then she smiled, raised her beautiful head, parted her lips . . . and blew . . . her . . . life . . . and all her beauty . . . away. Forever.

Just like a fool.

The devil slapped his knee, leaned back and laughed.

The Guardian Angel gave up. On its knees, beside the garden house door, it wept. The angel's voice was silenced by the golden pipe, the golden man. The golden pipe had a new voice to whisper in her ears. The Guardian Angel could only come back if she sought it. It will wait, even for nothing.

So . . . I'm just sittin here, lookin into this magic golden mirror Vanity has gave me because she could not bear to look into it anymore. She could not see the self she sought. The golden pipe has lied.

PLUS, I know she needed the money I pressed into her thin little hands. Almost all her beautiful things are gone . . . sold for that wisp of smoke. And that man she can never have for her own.

I am ponderin . . . ahhh, ponderin . . . thinkin about life . . . and death. Love.

Ahhhh, but so much happened. So much I didn't know about til way much later. My heart aches for her, but . . . it was HER choice, HER life.

In tryin to understand what had happened to my friend's mind, her life, I searched, asked questions of them people who knew her then, were her friends. Friends? I will tell you what I found out. It was pitiful. And if you got youngsters, you better listen to this first, then decide do you want them to hear this truth. This is just one day in the later life of Vanity, just fore she died from a heart attack, a broken, busted-heart attack.

Early one wintry morning after bein out all night til bout 5:00 A.M. . . . Vanity went inside the shell of her large, once beautiful house, empty now. Everything being sold, piece by piece. First, by Jody, then, at last, when her need was great and she started doin crack without Jody, she sold her own things, her own self. So the house was empty now.

The house note hadn't been paid in thirteen months and was soon to be foreclosed on. Gone. All her usta-be dreams. Gone.

The lectric company had turned off the lights. The gas company had done turned off the gas . . . and it was cold, cold, cold in that house. The water was the only thing on cause Jody knew how to turn it back on after the water company turned it off. So Vanity could drink water out a paper cup or a leftover tin can. Didn't need no water for cookin cause wasn't nothin to cook. She didn't have no appetite anyway for nothin but more crack . . . them bumps, them hits of rock. She was thin, thin, thin. Skin and bones. Somehow, she managed to keep her phone workin, cause she had to be able to get them calls from them fellows who might give her a bump. A Bump!

This particular night, and I know now there were lots of these kinda nights, she had been workin for that crack. She didn't call it "workin," but I do.

Jody was no longer the only man in her life. Now, she had had all kinds of men. All kinds. Kinds she wouldn't even use to spit on! Them "Bumps" had sucked and bumped all her pride out of her brain. That shit must be some powerful, cause you remember how full of pride she was!

Now . . . from the lowest person in a garbage can, man or woman, to the crack dealer who was the highest she could get, even they only wanted to use her for a half-hour or hour. Not even them so much anymore cause they had all already tore her down, stripped whatever little dignity she mighta had left. Yes, the bottom was as high as Vanity could go now. Them old days was gone. Like her beauty. Like her health. Like her life. Gone. No future to it.

Nothin meant nothin to her now but that next bump, that next rock. Low-life crack users called her a "Rock Star," laughin and graspin their crotches. I heard about em!

I give a lot of thought to the matter of Life. I mean to make mine as good and easy as possible. I stay as close to God and His wisdom as possible.

Some people say it takes courage to face the matter of death. Then . . . we are all courageous. Facing death, inevitably, to the end of our lives. Every day.

I believe it takes more courage to face Life. To survive the everyday matters of the mind, body, and heart. Every minute is of great moment in the matter of Life. There may be no small matters. A penny piece of lover can kill your soul. A person alive at two o'clock may be dead at two-ten, accidentally, from a wrong decision. A simple thing like boredom (which is really not simple) can create havoc in a life; it has the power to destroy. All in Life there is to decide upon is important to our living, in that it determines the quality, even the length, of our days.

Some people spend their lives in prisons.

Some, in the prison of drugs . . . or sex . . . alcohol . . . love-less unions . . . in hate . . . or greed . . . even sell themselves, their lives.

There is loneliness, losing and lack (and more).

There is love, laughter and longevity (and more).

Everyone wants to matter.

Everyone wants to know what the matter is.

So . . . I name this book what I believe.

That, always, no matter what the matter is . . .

THE MATTER IS LIFE.

RITA DOVE

RITA DOVE is currently Poet Laureate of the United States. A Pulitzer Prize–winning author, she has published five poetry collections, most recently *Grace Notes* (1989) and *Selected Poems* (1993), as well as a volume of short stories, the novel *Through the Ivory Gate* (1992), and the verse drama *The Darker Face of the Earth* (1994). Among her many honors are grants from the Guggenheim Foundation and the National Endowment for the Arts, the 1993 NAACP Award, and several honorary doctorates.

Ms. Dove received her B.A. from Miami University in Oxford, Ohio, in 1973 and her M.F.A. from the University of Iowa in 1977. She lives with her husband and daughter in Charlottesville, where she is Commonwealth Professor of English at the University of Virginia.

A WRITER IS A WRITER all the time. I am always thinking as a writer and trying to approach the world as a writer, which means using all of my senses all of the time—being open for the breeze that comes through the window, what it smells like, and what the trees look like when the breeze touches them. It can make for a pretty scattered impression on others. But that's how a writer lives—by being deeply in the world and being attuned to it a great deal of the time, while the rest of the time is spent in the actual writing and recollection of that interaction with the world.

When I was a kid I listened to stories—the women in the kitchen, Fourth of July cookouts, folks on the porch talking—I would eavesdrop really. Listening to these stories being told and how they would affect their listeners was quite an influence on my own desire to tell stories. I also did a lot of reading. As a child, my parents really opened me and my siblings up to the glory of reading and the infinite possibilities when you open a book. It was an activity that we could do practically any time—except at the dinner table. The library was the one place we could go to without asking permission. As long as we had finished the books we had taken out from our last trip there, we could go. And we always had.

My entire childhood was imbued with reading—afternoons of curling up with a book, and the pleasure of not knowing what was going to be in it until I opened it and began to read its words. The love I felt for the words on those pages made me want to create some words of my own, and to write the stories that I had not yet found.

When I began writing at maybe ten or eleven years old, it was wonderful, because I discovered that I could go wherever I wanted to go and do whatever I wanted to do. I didn't really tell anyone about it. My brother, who is a few years older than me, and I were very close as children. Every summer, we would have a newspaper, which I would usually quit about halfway through the summer to start my own newspaper. The title of my own newspaper usually made some reference to poetry. I remember one summer it was called *Poet's Delight*. Other than my brother, I really didn't show anyone what I wrote, not even my friends. It wasn't shame, it was just that writing was such an intimate act for me that it didn't really occur to me to bring it out into the world all that much.

When I got to high school, my English teacher brought a few of us to a book signing one afternoon. I hadn't shown her any of my writing either, beyond my English papers. The writer at the book signing was John Ciardi, the poet and translator. I was so amazed that writers were really *people*. At that moment, I realized that this "activity" I had been doing, that I had been thinking of as somewhat of a game—some game that I would one day have to put away in order to become an adult—that this activity was really something adults did and were respected for. And it was called writing.

I did not make the conscious decision to become a writer until I was in college. It wasn't until I realized that I was rearranging my schedule to fit in creative writing courses that I thought, Well, maybe I should make a go of this, because writing had obviously become the most important thing to me. I was then able to recognize the yearning that I felt inside, the joy that I got when I wrote something I felt was halfway decent. When I was able to understand that the joy could somehow satisfy the yearning, I realized that the yearning, the joy, and the satisfaction were about wanting to write. I think I had the yearning for a long time before recognizing it; I just didn't know what it was.

In my poetry, I write about what the weather is like, or what the sand feels like under a sandal—that kind of thing—and it may be drawn from an experience that I have had, or that someone I know has had. I draw from other people quite a lot, particularly family members. *Thomas and Beulah* is a good example of that because it began with a story that my grandmother told me about my grandfather. As I began to re-create the scene, the event that she told me about, imagination came in. I hadn't been there, and she hadn't been there either—only my grandfather had been there, and he had long since passed away—so by necessity I had to use my imagination. In imagining, I also put my own feelings into it—how I would have felt had I actually been there—all the while trying to slip into my grandfather's skin.

As that book of poetry grew, I went to the library and did research to find out things—like what Akron, Ohio, was like in the twenties. I also talked with my mother and drew on her memories, and then I sometimes just plain made things up. That's how I work. I did the same thing with my novel *Through the Ivory Gate*—I have played the cello, but I've never been a puppeteer— so it becomes a wonderful kind of mix, and I really don't try and sort it out that much.

I do think quite a few writers work in this same way; when we try to talk about that magical moment when the poem or the story or the scene takes off and comes alive, I know that for me it's a feeling of trying to write just to keep up with that moment. This moment is the point when all of the things I just mentioned—the memories, the imagination, the stories I've heard—all come together in such a unified piece that I don't know where the energy is coming from and all I can do is ride with it. It feels terrific. It is so exhilarating, I feel like I could write forever, that I am inexhaustible. The ideas and the words come faster than I can write them down. Although sometimes, right before that happens, there is a moment of great despair when things don't seem to be clicking; but the faith that it will come together takes me there. I learn so much in the process; it is profound discovery.

There is some truth to the whole notion that something strikes the poet like a thunderbolt and she is then inspired. Inspiration is part of the writing process, and I think of it as being much more visceral than cerebral. I also think that there is a different kind of inspiration that comes when one is working and things begin to click together. I'll leave it up to all the scientists and psychologists to come up with the right terminology for it, but I do think that I try to engage all of my senses when I write. Absolutely and completely. I try to get *in* it. And then I need to find a word that will best describe being in it, which is very cerebral. The mind, the soul, the heart, and the heartbeat try to get into sync, and when they do, it is very difficult to say which takes precedence, in fact I don't think any one thing does.

When the writing doesn't gel together, I just keep working. For example, since I am both a poet and a fiction writer, let me try to explain the differences I feel between both mediums. I find that the rhythms are very different between these two genres. With poetry, very often there are the days and hours of a lot of frustration when things are not coming together. When things finally do click, I find the moments of connection are usually much more brilliant and unequivocal. With prose, I find that the periods when things are not clicking are not quite as depressing because there is so much to do in prose besides working on those connections. I guess you could call it housekeeping—tidying up ragged paragraphs, creating an atmosphere, checking dialogue— so that I can keep active in the work and not despair that it won't come together. Maybe it is because I consider myself more of a poet than a fiction writer, but I also find the moments that come together in prose are not as epiphanal as those in poetry. So it's a trade-off. I prefer the higher highs and the deeper depths in poetry.

For me, there is simply a deep and basic pleasure in seeing words come alive. The simpler the word, the better. Because words are amazingly compact; they carry so much power in such a small package. I think the simpler the word, the more power it contains, because our first words were very simple, one-syllable words. If I can find a way to bring back all the power of the word *bread*, not Wonder bread, but *bread*—the stuff that gives us life— if I can restore the freshness and magic to that word in a prose passage or in a poem, then I've got it all. What an incredible power—I smell it, I feel it, I am alive.

I run through all the different attributes of a word when I am trying to find the right one. A word not only has a meaning—it also has a sound, a feeling in the mouth, a texture, a history. Very often, if a word has the right meaning, but not the sense, the deeper sense I need, I try to think of words that rhyme, or I look up its etymology. Writing for me means that intense pleasure of dealing with language, working with the language like a potter works with clay. I think most writers have an almost shameless love of language, of words and the way they work.

When we are children, we love to play with language; we like feeling sounds in our mouth. Then as we start to grow up, what begins to happen is that the pleasure of mouthing words has to be compromised because words are also used for daily interactions. Using charcoal or paint to create art is an activity that can be kept discrete. But the use of words can't be. We have to use them to talk and to communicate. Many people forget the pleasure of words for the purpose of expediency—they have to get on with their lives. I also think that this is why a lot of poets and writers are not great conversationalists. We are not the kind of people who sit around at the party spouting off witty and glib repartee. And a lot of that has to do with this intense love of words. To constantly make the switch between honoring every word and using them just to get on with things is very difficult. It's almost schizophrenia.

I've recently been named poet laureate of the nation, and I am still trying to decide what that title means. It is a kind of public or outward affirmation, not so much that I'm a good writer, but that the writing reaches an audience. And that is gratifying. Unless you do a lot of public readings, every time you sit down to write or finish a piece, there is that fear of being misunderstood. You say to yourself: What I'm writing is *really* crazy; no one is going to relate to this. So to have this sort of official recognition not only as a poet and writer, but also as someone who can stand forward and be a channel for literature in this country, is marvelous.

It doesn't really matter to me what kind of validation the title may give me as a poet—I don't really worry about that kind of stuff. Every time I sit down to write, it's a new ball game. The poem, or the story, or the scene, that I'm working on has its own problems, and there is always the fear that the poem or passage will not work or mean anything to anyone else. The intensity of this sort of hand-to-hand combat never goes away.

It is very exciting to think that the country thinks enough about literature to appoint a younger poet laureate, which may encourage the idea of writing in children and engage our youth by saying in effect: See? This can be done. That the country chose to honor a black woman is also tremendously exciting. On the one hand, it declares that there is value and richness in diversity. But it also shows that multiculturalism and diversity do not mean being separate. My ultimate desire is to be considered as part of the human family—to be recognized and respected as a black woman, but not to have that fact make any earth-shaking difference. It is significant that I am a black women, but it is not the end-all-be-all in terms of being poet laureate.

As a black woman writer, I recognize that there are powers that may choose not to consider me as part of the human family. This is no reason not to make the writing as honest as I possibly can. In other words, if the character who I'm writing about is a black woman, I don't feel compelled to present her in a good light. If you want people to recognize and honor the individuality and humanity of each person, each character must be rendered as an individual and as human, with faults, and doubts, and all those kinds of things. It is difficult to show a character's faults when you know that there are people who already think of African-American women as lesser beings, but it is absolutely essential that you do. Otherwise the character becomes cardboard. And what is not real is not honest.

There is a friend of mine, Marilyn Waniek, a black woman poet who was nominated for a National Book Award a few years back. We became really close correspondents long before we met. She has a book of poems called *The Homeplace* that deal with her family, and in the copy she gave me she had written: "To the sister I never had." Now, she has a sister; that wasn't the point. Her inscription encapsulated the feeling I have about other black women writers out there—they are all the sisters I never had, even though I have two sisters. They complete the family. The family of black women. It is an incredible feeling, not being alone.

When I was in graduate school, I would go the library and wander around picking out books. One day I was in the stacks, and I noticed this one book. The library had removed all the book jackets so this book was a sort of dark grayish black, and on its binding the title in bright letters: *The Bluest Eye*. I didn't recognize the writer, but I took the book down from the shelf and started reading. From the very first page, I felt that this was a sister I did not know. I assumed the writer was a woman because of the way *"Toni"* was spelled, but I had had no premonition whether she was black or not. The writing gave me this incredible visceral sensation, almost like hunger, so I kept reading and the feeling got deeper and deeper. Since then, I have often felt that way about other black women writers—as though we are all drinking out of the same well, that there is enough water for everybody, and what a wonderful place to meet.

For a few weeks it would be tolerable: a cube of a room, white walls, white floorboards, daybed with a blue coverlet. A dinette set with two straight-back chairs, the kitchen no more than a counter. Virginia had been expecting a dank linoleum-lined room in a motel complex, or worse, a room in the home of concerned parents, not this postmodern artist's garret built over a languishing shoe repair shop. Venetian blinds shaded the huge windows along the wall that fronted the street. It was actually a miniature studio; whoever had decorated it—a photographer, perhaps?—had used white paint to extend the cramped space, as if the walls were nothing more than reflected light that could squeeze through the slits in the blinds and pick up a few flashes from the stingy scribble of the canal in the background, lifting over the tire factories in the east to be absorbed finally into the chalky sky.

She decided to shower first. She must have seemed like a maniac, rolling into the school parking lot a day early, bleary-eyed and wrinkled like a bum. What did they think of her—Mrs. Peck, Ludwig, the cook, Jean Gilroy?

She started toward the bathroom but stopped at the cello in the middle of the floor, daylight warming along the gray curve of its vinyl case. She had not played seriously since college. Accompanying the troupe's performances and clowning around as Parker picked out old Beatles songs on the piano didn't count—that wasn't *real* music, music that made you forget where you were, made you forget where your arms and legs ended and luscious sound began.

She had started playing the cello when she was nine, shortly after the move to Arizona. At the beginning of the school year in Akron, every child in fourth grade had been issued a pre-instrument called a tonette so the teacher could determine who had an "aptitude" for music. Virginia had liked the neatness of the tonette, its modest musical range and how it fit into her school desk on the right side. Whenever she covered a fingerhole, she felt the contour of its slightly raised lip and imagined she was playing the tentacle of an octopus.

She had chafed through months of scales and simple songs, waiting for the moment when she would walk across the auditorium stage and choose: kneel among the rows of somber black cases, undo the metal clasps and fling open the lid to reveal her instrument, a flute or a clarinet, glowing softly, half buried in deep blue velvet.

But before she could make her choice, they moved to Arizona. There, the music instruments were stored in a classroom trailer, and when she opened the flute case she nearly winced from the glare bouncing off all that polished silver, those gloating caps and hinges. The clarinet was worse—it looked like an overdesigned walking stick, sounded like a clown laughing, and had reeds that needed to be softened in spit.

The music teacher shut the cases with a succession of curt clicks. "That leaves the strings," she sighed, leading the way back through the noonday blaze and into the main building, where the violins, violas, cellos and double basses were housed. There, by virtue of its sonorous name, Virginia asked for the violoncello—and was too intimidated by the teacher's growing impatience to protest when what emerged from the back closets was something resembling not a guitar, but a childsized android. In her anguish Virginia bowed her head and blindly accepted the instrument. It was not long, however, before she realized that she had made a good choice, for the sound of its name was synonymous with the throbbing complaint that poured out of its cumbersome body.

It took her nearly a year just to learn how to hold it properly. She had been accustomed to practicing after school, but one weekend evening while her parents were out, she dragged the instrument into their bedroom and used pillows to prop the music on the armchair. She was just about to sit on the edge of the bed when something, maybe the shadow thrown from the flowered lampshade or the slats of light sifting from the street, made her want to *do things right*. She got a straight-back chair from the dining room and sat down correctly, bringing the instrument slowly toward her body. The lamp picked up the striations down the back of the wood, each strip slightly different, a little browner, a little more golden, but meeting its mate at the spine, a barely perceptible seam. For the first time she saw that the back of the cello was rounded like a belly, the belly of a tiger she had to bring close to her, taming it before she was torn limb from limb. She had to love and not be scared, and show the cat that it did not need to growl to protect itself. The animal stood on its hind legs and pressed its torso to hers, one paw curled like a ribbon behind her left ear. It was heavy; she sat very straight in the chair in order to support it.

Funny how fantasy works. And memory. I haven't thought about that evening in years. Virginia bent down and lay the cello case on its back, trying, as she knelt to unsnap the metal clasps, to ignore the musk that wafted up; but then she became aware of the dried sweat filming her skin, and the way her stockings had sagged into gritty puddles in her shoes. She stood up and made for the shower.

Virginia gasped in relief at the first gush of hot water on her back. Ah, the pleasure of getting clean! She closed her eyes so as to dissolve in the slipstream, breathing in the steamy clamor of chlorine and almond-scented lather.

Clayton never touched the cello without washing his hands first; more often than not, he'd change his shirt before going to the university orchestra rehearsal. "One must honor the art," he said. "Marcel Proust donned formal attire before sitting down to write *Remembrance of Things Past*."

It had been impossible to miss him that first day of rehearsal. Even from the fourth stand, Virginia could make out the back of his head wafting on the chestnut-colored stem of his neck. *A brother in the cello section—second chair at that!* She leaned over the music stand to get a better view.

Her stand partner sniffed and turned his instrument away, hunching his shoulder as if she was about to bump his raggedy wooden matchbox. For auditions, she had chosen a slow passage from the D Minor Corelli Sonata, hoping the melodic line would camouflage her rusty technique. The sight-reading portion hadn't been too bad, probably because she'd been so relaxed about the whole thing. Her only ambition had been to sit in the back of the orchestra and deposit her modest tones into that gorgeous cornucopia of sound spilling out all around her. No one was more surprised than she when she was positioned before several music majors. She could feel them seething behind her—especially her partner who, as inside stand member, would have to turn all pages.

Who was this dude sitting up on first stand as casual as you pleased? Most black musicians she had met before were either horn men—saxophonists of every stripe, and that lean, arrogant trumpeter from L.A.—or the ubiquitous percussionists who were always clicking out rhythms with their tongues and drumming on tabletops. She hated to fall into stereotyping, but it was true.

At the end of rehearsal the principal cellist, a stocky redheaded guy named Paul, stood up to introduce the new section members. When it was Virginia's turn, Clayton lifted an eyebrow and bowed slightly. Then there was pandemonium as eighty-odd musicians, using their instrument cases as battering rams, stormed the exit.

Heart thudding, she threaded her way through the thicket of music stands to the doorway where he stood chatting with the principal cellist. Paul clapped her on the shoulder in a hale-and-hearty manner. "Welcome to the salt mines, Virginia." He grinned and took off, whistling: *Heigh-ho, heigh-ho, it's off to work we go*. She turned to look up at Clayton, who seemed in no hurry to follow.

He was tall, about six feet four; his nose was flat *and* sharp, like Benin bronzes, with a prominent ridge and flaring nostrils. An Omar Sharif mustache straggled over his lips, and there was a hint of a cleft in the rather small chin. Had he been waiting for her? The thought made her dizzy.

"Yes, indeed. Welcome. My name is Clayton Everett."

She nodded. "Thanks. I mean, it's great to be able to play in an orchestra again."

"Oh?" There he went lifting that eyebrow. "Haven't you played in a while?"

"I've been taking private lessons with Kadinski, but this is the first semester I've been able to work orchestra into my schedule."

He held the door open and started down the hall toward the cello room, moving along with an off-kilter camel's lope. Every music major had a locker, but cellists and bassists also had a key to humidified rooms where the larger instruments were stored.

"Mr. Kadinski's my teacher also. What are you working on now?"

"The Concerto in D by Anton Kraft. I'd never heard of him before, but the piece is really wonderful."

"Kraft!" he exclaimed. "I had to locate that concerto for my library-science class. We were given obscure compositions to track down, and Anton Kraft was my final exam question last semester." He paused, shifting his cello case to the other hand. "I've never had a chance to find a recording of it. Would you play it for me?"

They had stopped in front of a practice room. Panicked, Virginia stammered, "I'm not a music major."

"That's no reason."

"And I've just started the Kraft." It was a lie, and they both knew it. "Give me a few weeks to get it under my belt, and I'll play it for you."

"Is that a promise?"

"Promise."

He set the cello case down and extended his hand, smiling. The dry warmth of his grip, the tender amusement in his eyes, quietly destroyed her—and the way he spoke, with a deliberate, almost decorous, formulation of the phrases. He reached for the doorknob to the practice room.

"You're going to practice? Now?" she said, bewildered.

"Sure. After orchestra is the perfect time; the muscles are all warmed up."

She had never heard of anyone practicing *after* three hours of orchestra! Even with the frequent breaks during the rehearsal (the French horns were awful and the conductor had to stop and concentrate on their part), her arm was ready to drop off by the time they were given the sign to pack up.

"What are you working on?" she asked meekly.

"The Lalo. And I would be pleased to play it for you in a few

weeks, when I've gotten it under *my* belt. Good evening, Virginia."
He bowed his ridiculous but somehow appropriate bow again, and
went inside.

She'd met lots of crazy musicians, but no one like Clayton. He was
as obsessed as the others, but he had a quirky sense of humor, a
slow ironic counterpoint to his own beliefs. And he didn't look
quite like anyone else. First of all, he didn't look very black. He
didn't look white either, or Puerto Rican. He wore his hair parted
dangerously near the middle and combed in little ripples like Cab
Calloway, though sometimes he let it fly up a bit at the ends in def-
erence to the campus pressure for Afros. His caramel-colored skin
darkened to toffee under fluorescent light but sometimes took on a
golden sheen, especially in the vertical shafts of sunlight that
poured into his favorite practice room where she'd often peeked in
on him—an uncanny complexion, as if the shades swirled just
under the surface.

Virginia's friends gave her advice on how to get him. "You two
can play hot duets together," they giggled.

As it turned out, she didn't have to plan a thing. She was reading John Hawkes's *Blood Oranges* for Twentieth-Century Lit one
afternoon in the courtyard of the Fine Arts Building when the
sunny day turned suddenly cold. If she went all the way back to the
dorm for a sweater, she'd be late for orchestra rehearsal. So she
stuck it out for a quarter of an hour, until a few minutes before
rehearsal at four. By that time her fingers were so stiff, she had to
run them under hot water to loosen them up. Then she hurried to
the cello room, where all the instruments were lined up like novi-
tiates; she felt a strange reverence every time she stepped across the
threshold into its cool serenity. There they stood, obedient yet

voluptuous in their molded cases. In the dim light their plump forms looked sadly human, as if they were waiting for something better to come along but knew it wouldn't.

Virginia grabbed her cello and was halfway down the hall when she realized she'd forgotten to leave her books behind. She decided against turning back and continued to the basement, where the five-till-four pandemonium was breaking loose. Clayton was stuffing his books into his locker, the music major's privilege.

"Hey, Clayton, how's it going?"

As if it were routine, he took her books and wedged them in next to his. They started toward the orchestra hall. Virginia cast a surreptitious glance upward; five minutes to four or not, Clayton was not rushing. His long, gangling frame seemed to be held together by molasses; he moved deliberately, negotiating the crush while humming a tricky passage from Schumann, sailing along above the mob.

After rehearsal she reminded him that her books were in his locker.

"I think I'll go practice," he said. "Would you like to listen?"

"I'll miss dinner," she replied, and was about to curse herself for her honesty when he said, "I have cheese and soup back at the fraternity house, if you don't mind the walk."

The walk was twenty minutes of agonizing bliss, with the wind off the lake whipping her blue, and Clayton too involved with analyzing the orchestra's horn section to notice. When they reached the fraternity house, a brick building with a crumbling porch and white pillars and weeds cracking the front path, she was nearly frozen through. He heated up a can of Campbell's Split Pea with Ham and plunked the cheese down in the center of the dinette table.

"It's not much," he apologized, but she was thinking *A loaf of bread, a jug of wine,* and felt sated before lifting the first spoonful.

The house was rented to Alpha Phi Alpha, one of the three black fraternities on campus. It had the musty tennis-shoes-and-ripe-laundry smell of bachelor rooms, combined with the intensely sweet scent of oil essences she'd first encountered in a head shop David Goldstein, her brother's friend, had taken her to—patchouli, vanilla bean, cinnamon. Books and jackets were strewn everywhere, dishes piled in the sink.

"When did you begin playing?" she asked.

"I began late, I'm afraid," Clayton replied. "Ninth grade. But I felt at home immediately. With the music, I mean. The instrument took a little longer. Everyone said I was too tall to be a cellist." He grimaced.

Virginia watched him as he talked. He was the same golden brown as his instrument, and his mustache followed the lines of the cello's scroll.

"So what did you do?" she asked.

"Whenever my height came up, I would say, 'Remember the bumblebee.' "

"What do bumblebees have to do with cellos?"

"The bumblebee, aerodynamically speaking, is too large for flight. But the bee has never heard of aerodynamics, so it flies in spite of the laws of gravity. I merely wrapped my legs and arms around the cello and kept playing."

Music was the only landscape in which he seemed at ease. In that raunchy kitchen, elbows propped on either side of the cooling soup, he was fidgety, even a little awkward. But when he sat up behind his instrument, he had the irresistible beauty of someone who had found his place.

Virginia stepped out of the shower and rubbed down until her skin burned, then soothed it with cocoa-butter lotion. Refreshed, nearly pristine, she sat down in the dinette chair that wobbled the least and pulled the cello to her. Now, for the first time since Clayton, she was trying to make music again. Haydn? Elgar? *Tiger, tiger, burning bright* . . . Her fingers found the opening measures on their own volition, those triadic arpeggios of the First Bach Suite that sounded like warm-up scales until the gradual modulations of the high notes in each phrase insinuated themselves into her blood: above the treadmill of chordal progressions a luminous melody unscrolling and floating away, high in the upper ether, where there was no memory or hurt.

GLORIA

WADE-GAYLES

G

LORIA WADE-GAYLES, a native of Memphis, Tennessee, earned her B.A. at LeMoyne College, her M.A. at Boston University, and her Ph.D. at Emory University. She has received several fellowships and research awards, among them Woodrow Wilson, Southern Education Foundation, the Mellon, and DuBois Fellows' Appointment at Harvard University. In addition to poetry and scholarly essays, she has published three books: *No Crystal Stair: Race and Sex in Black Women's Novels, 1946–76* (1983); a book of poetry, *Anointed to Fly* (1991); and *Pushed Back to Strength: A Black Woman's Journey Home* (1993). *Moving in my Heart,* an anthology of writings on black women's spirituality, is being published by Beacon Press in 1995. Wade-Gayles is revising a second volume of poetry and working on her first novel. Named 1991 CASE Professor for the State of Georgia, she is professor of English and women's studies at Spelman College. Wade-Gayles is the mother of two children.

WRITING SIMPLY IS. In the same way that being alive is about breathing, being alive for me is about writing. Writing is the way I express my feelings and my dreams. It is the way I communicate with people. It is the way for me to reach inside myself and pull out what I am feeling and thinking. Writing simply is. It is an expression of my "who-ness." I use writing to clarify, to excavate, to analyze, to emote, to make connections, to remember. It is my main medium. And that is why I consider myself a writer. I have made a commitment to the written word.

Through writing I have excavated my socialization as a black woman growing up in a segregated South, how I have felt about myself throughout my life, and how I feel about myself now. I have excavated "African-American Cultural Phenomenon" that I can't find in the media, or in a printed book, but only in my mind. When I excavate these sorts of experiences, I bring them up and out, and onto paper. I turn them around, I stroke them, I see them, I feel them, I smell them, and I hear them. These experiences become real for me and help me to shape a view of myself, of my people, of the world really.

Sometimes the feelings, the memories, and the ideas come to me in the strangest and most unlikeliest of moments—driving down the expressway, on my way to the library, or to the grocery store, or when I am sleeping, or eating. I may hear a voice, see or feel something from the past that is related to the now moment, and I am claimed by it. I am claimed by these experiences that insist on being written. Often I rush to write them down, and later I translate, because when I write them down at first they are only recognizable to me.

The balance between my feelings as a writer, and the everydayness of my life is difficult. It is a trick done with mirrors and puffs of smoke. Writing is something I feel I have to do. I am disciplined around it. I say to myself, Here are two things you must do—you can't say no to writing, and you can't say no to teaching. So I cut out other things, like television, long phone conversations, and many social activities in order to create time for both things. That doesn't eliminate room for love and relationships. I don't think one can connect with one's self unless one is able to love and be involved in relationships. But every day I must give some time to my writing. And from that, I get a sense of accomplishment, a sense of achievement, a feeling that I have been responsible, that I have not denied a part of myself. The reward is feeling that I have given birth to a feeling that was inside of me and wanted to come out, to be seen and heard and validated and embraced. Of course there will always be experiences still inside that I haven't yet heard, that is the very nature of the creative process. There is no end to what writers can write about.

There is a theory that all fictive writing is largely autobiographical. I would say that 60 percent of my writing is. But we need to define the term "autobiographical." My writing is autobiographical in the sense that it is about experiences that I have had personally, and also in the sense that it is about experiences that I know have happened to other people. I don't think the creative process allows you to differentiate between what is imagination and what is reality. Often, we are not as in control of the creative process as we think we are. So that which is imagined and that which is real blend together to create something very special, and something that is in its own way very real. And that is a difficult point to come to.

Right now, I am working on a novel that is about three black women in their fifties who for different reasons have been celibate, and who, also for different reasons, have decided to come out of their celibacy. The story is layered in complexity. It is a hard story to write about because I find myself listening to the voices of women who are in pain, some who I have known personally, others who I have heard about. I struggle with that pain, because I don't want to simplify being celibate, and I don't want to make it too complex. To be woman and to be black, and to be aware of being both, causes us to look at every experience with very, very careful eyes. We are caught between not wanting to divide the two and trying to create a medium that is sensitive to both without minimizing either. Involving sexuality adds a whole separate dimension.

In this novel, I want to reflect the reality of black women in their fifties dealing with their senses of self, during this particular era. It is a response to sexism, it is an expression of a black woman's right and need for help to claim herself physically, to embrace her sensuality. Celibacy could be a black woman's rejection of her sexuality or of her sexual myth, although that is not my intention. The novel is about black women coming into their wholeness and recognizing that embracing their sexuality is a healthy thing.

My childhood is the easiest experience for me to write about. In spite of some struggles, it was a very positive time, a time that I can and do celebrate. I had a *phenomenal* mother and was immersed in love. My mother was a self-affirmed woman, a womanist, long before we used the term. She was very much her own person. Writing about my childhood is a marvelous way of remaining connected to her. Writing about my childhood is also a way of giving my son and daughter a gift that will help them understand what I have done for them, as their mother-friend, is really a manifestation of what I received as a child. My mother gave me profound belief in self, in love, and in giving. She taught me to remain connected to my spiritual self, to reject materialism as a definition of success, and to have an inner joy. Spirituality appears in every shape that we assume as human beings. I don't think that there is any experience, any role, any achievement, any place, in which we find ourselves where there is not spirituality.

The first black woman writer who had a profound affect on me was Ann Petry. I am very interested in class and the struggles of inner-city people, what we call the "underprivileged," because I grew up in a housing project. Petry's sensitivity to the symbiotic relationship among race, gender, and class in her portrayal of Lutie (from *The Street*) is absolutely brilliant. That a writer could bring all of that into one space and move a reader to see what was happening was truly amazing to me.

I was also greatly moved by Nella Larsen because of her treatment of color. I come from a family with people on both sides of the rainbow. My paternal family has very dark skin, and my maternal family is what we call "high yaller." So I grew up very aware of the struggle of fair-skinned black women. My mother, my grandmother, and my aunt would talk about those problems when I was growing up. In fact, my grandmother "Passed." She lived in a black community, but she passed in order to go to the white world, get what the white world had to offer, and then bring it back to the black community. I found Nella Larsen's treatment of color and of commitment to black people inspirational.

I feel connected to Alice Walker because of her spirituality, her courage, and her daring approach to reality. She is also southern and came from an underprivileged background that she never denied. Her background becomes raw material for her art, through which I see her doing a kind of excavation. I have seen Alice Walker spiraling since her first novel, *The Third Life of*

Grange Copeland, and she has continued spiraling upward, upward, moving toward the very cosmos. Her interest in what we, who are disconnected from the spiritual world, are doing to the material world, to trees, to water, to air, to other people, is tremendous. She has truly been an inspiration to me.

Mari Evans wrote a poem called "I'm a Black Woman," and what has stayed with me from that poem throughout my experience as a black woman writer is this—"Tall/indestructible/impervious/define time/space/look on me/and be renewed." That to me is one of the most brilliant and profound statements about black women, and I am renewed every day when I look at the black women and the black women writers around me.

Being black and woman means being aware that I have experiences that are unique. It means being aware that I am connected, historically, to black men, and always keeping that in focus, never looking exclusively at my race/gender and forgetting my race. That is particularly important to me as the mother of a son, and also as the daughter of a father. My awareness of the historical and spiritual connection that I have with black men does not mean I feel an obligation to be loyal to them. My sense of family came from my family. As simple as that sounds, I grew up in a very loving, closely knit family, which I wrote about in my book *Pushed Back to Strength*. We are anchored in family, in community, and in race.

I teach truth. And when I tell people that, they say, "Well you teach literature, that's fiction, that's not truth." I teach African-American Literature, with an emphasis on African-American Women's Literature. My philosophy as a teacher is the same as my philosophy as a person, and that is—whatever you do, you do it with passion and you do it without apology. So I teach passionately. I make demands on students without apology. I share my feelings without apology. I challenge text and theories without apology. I embrace my people's history and my people's literature. And passion for me is both visceral and cerebral. I think we are both body and soul at all times. To think in terms of a duality, as western culture does, is dangerous and destructive of the whole self.

When you own something or celebrate something, you do so all the time. And if you don't, you are not really owning it or celebrating it. The presence of white students in my classes when I am celebrating my Africanity, my womanness, does not alter the celebration. As a matter of fact, what I have found is that most white students who are enrolled in black studies classes bring to those classes a desire, a genuine desire to learn about black experience. As a result, they tend to anticipate the sort of celebration in which we are involved, but whether they do or not is of no interest to me. The truth is the truth no matter who the audience is, and the truth for me is an embracing of my history, my culture, and my self.

One of the reasons I believe I write is that I want that which is disappearing in African-American culture to be available for generations to come. That which has sustained us as a people, claimed us as a people, to be in books. Writing is perhaps my way of stopping time and yet moving ahead in time. At this moment in time, this is what was happening, this was what was beautiful and ugly, joyous and painful, and once I have stopped to see that, I can move ahead. A miracle for me is the emotional and spiritual health of black people, within the family, within the community, and outside in our own personal world. That for me is a miracle, and I want it in writing.

From
ANOINTED TO FLY
Anointed to Fly
A Poem for Young Sojourners

creme
straight creme mixed with
   cinnamon
churned like butter creme

and **tan**

coffee tan
smooth cocoa tan
dusty tan
like the wings on a mourning
   dove
in flight tan

and **brown**

brown like the arms of warrior
   trees
that refused the rope
brown like fertile fields
unfurrowed unploughed
caramel brown
chestnut brown
chocolate brown

and **yellow**

high yellow
lemon yellow
butterscotch yellow
don't-have-to-defend-myself
   yellow

and **Black**

panther black
midnight black
intense black
singing freedom black
like won't be diluted grey black

black women
our sisters

we know you well.

you are the
daughters of women
who dipped you whole
in the waters of promise.

you have no achilles heels.

for you are the
daughters of women
who detached their wings
repaired them
and passed them on
to you
that you would fly
soar
like eaglewomen black
beyond the reach
of anyone who wants us buried
again

with hands that cupped breast
    for you
they cut the cord
unfurled your wings
released you
and in their woman's voice
they are chanting to the winds
    you ride,
"Not Fragile"
Not Fragile
Not Fragile
Not Fragile
but "Handle with care"

we know you well

we see you pirouetting like first
picks for an Alvin Ailey suite on
    blackness

promenading
strutting
strolling
high-stepping
gliding
walking big-city tough
small-town shy
walking in footprints
you can not yet measure
but must claim as heirlooms
from women
who are legends
and legacies
which name you
black women

we know you well

you are black women
preening with pride
palpitating with passion
stretching for knowledge

empowered empowering Black
    women
Black chosen women
our sisters
anointed to fly

we know you well

you have come
   from ranch-styles
   split-levels
   estates that own the woods
you have come
   from duplexes
   with walls thin enough
   to stereo sounds of sorrow
you have come
   from tenements shot-guns
      flats projects
   sharecroppers' borrowed
      rooms
   that were/are oven-warm
      with love.

we know you well

before your coming
we stroked your tight-skinned
   young faces
we touched the center of your
   tears
we stretched your tender
   muscles into smiles
we danced like African queens
   to the rhythm of
   your joys
we blended the chords of your
   symphony song

and we charted the trajectory of
   your dreams
across the heavens

like meteors knowing their
   destination
your dreams will light up the
   darkness
and from their cradles
flowers will bloom

we know you well

black women before us
who were daughters of black
   women
who were daughters of black
   women
who were sister of sisters
black women
African women
the womb of civilization

taught us to breathe in your
   breath
to stay alive for you
to tighten the drum for you
to open the books for you
to hand the gavel to you
to move the pen for you
to give the world to you

and your women's hands
must change it

we know you well

you have come find the answers
we give only the questions

you have to come to begin your
    planting season
we will place your hands in the
    soil

you must dig
you must plant
you must till
you must harvest
the fullest yield
of your blackness
your womanness
your genius
and pass it on

to

black women
our sisters
all sisters
all people
everywhere

whom you must
anoint to fly.

NIKKI

GIOVANNI

NIKKI GIOVANNI, one of America's most widely read living poets, has earned a reputation for being outspoken and controversial—mostly because she always speaks her mind. She entered the literary world at the height of the Black Arts Movement and quickly achieved not simple fame but stardom. A recording of her poems was one of the best-selling albums in the country; all but one of her nearly twenty books are still in print, with several having sold more than a hundred thousand copies. Named woman of the year by three different magazines, including *Ebony,* and recipient of a host of honorary doctorates and awards, Nikki Giovanni has read from her work and lectured at colleges around the country. Her books include *Black Feeling, Black Talk/Black Judgement; My House; The Women and the Men; Cotton Candy on a Rainy Day; Those Who Ride the Night Winds;* and *Sacred Cows . . . and Other Edibles* (all available in Quill/William Morrow editions). Nikki Giovanni received her B.A. in 1967 from Fisk University and is a professor of English at Virginia Polytechnic.

'M A POET. And I write. I think we make too much out of writing as a profession. We tend to make it into something mystical, and it really isn't. I happened to have an interest in people. I am a black writer and I write a lot about black people. I think that that is not only legitimate, but necessary. I enjoy what I do. There will always be varying degrees of financial or critical success based on who's giving the prizes or the money, but I think as a writer, you have to say, "Do I want to do this?" It's not really a job. The writing itself, without being mystical about it, is an art, or a calling, but it should really be something that you want to do, something that you would do no matter what.

Here in America we have many, many writers, and probably even more poets. We have many, many poets who are also writers, but nobody knows it, as if somehow poetry isn't writing, which is regrettable. But for lack of a better word, the hierarchy of writing is that first we have the oral story that gets told, and then we have the poem. After that comes the short story, and then the embellishment that the novel brings. So poetry is really at the heart of writing. And I like being there.

My poetry comes from interest. I am interested in my people, and in contemporary issues. I like the past, but I am totally fascinated by the future. So I'm always trying to pin down the present, because if you can pin down the present you're going to get a pretty good idea of where the future is. When I was growing up, I wasn't encouraged to write, but I also wasn't discouraged. Nobody said, "You can't do that." I went to all segregated schools in the South as a child. I think that everybody, my parents, my grandparents, my grandmother especially, because she would listen to me, and all of my teachers, were encouraging, not specifically to Nikki, but to people. I attended a private Episcopal elementary school, and my class was small, we had maybe fourteen or fifteen students. My mother is here visiting me now, and we were just recently talking about the people who came out of that class. I realized that out of that class, there is a very high number of people who are doing, if not what they want to do, at least doing something very well, and are fairly successful. If everybody is doing well, I have to figure it wasn't just me who was being encouraged, and that the environment was good. Not necessarily for writing, but for living.

I write from the first-person singular, which is a style I share with a number of other writers, but my writing is not as autobiographical as people think. What I try to do is take on a persona. Some things are specific to me and my experience, but most things are really not. It's about empathy. School just started up—I teach creative writing—and one of the things I really try to work on with my students is empathy. We have a "word of the day," and I bet that in any one semester, out of its sixteen weeks, the "word of the day" will be *empathy* for at least ten of those weeks. Because you have to empathize to be a writer. The way that I have learned empathy, and the way that I teach it, is by saying, "Does that make sense to me/you? Would I/you do that?" If you were in that position, would you do that? You've got to put yourself in your characters' shoes.

One of the things I really wanted to capture in my earlier writing was to express the reality of a people. I wanted to make a statement for a people who didn't have a voice, and that was a combination of empathy and personal, specific experiences. I think I was historically concurrent, and conscious of it, with people who wrote the spirituals and people who wrote the blues—we were all trying to make a statement for a people who didn't have a voice. And although black people have been freed during my lifetime, although we have alleviated a level of overt segregation, that does not mean America is wonderful, it just means that there are no "Colored Waiting Rooms" or "Colored Drinking Fountains." And although, now, black people really can say what we need to say most of the time, previously, I wanted to try to be as much of a voice as I possibly could for everyone.

My writing has since become more for me and my own personal interests. And that is important, otherwise I'd end up wanting people to be oppressed so that I could have a job. I don't believe in that. As I see our people have come to being able to express themselves, I have narrowed my writing so that I become *one* of the voices, not *the* voice.

My favorite thing about words is the weight that they can carry. I'm a minimalist writer, and so I'm always trying to figure out what word can carry half a ton without being some crazy big word. A word is like a snail, what the snail carries on its back should be proportionate to Atlas movin' the earth. I think words should be able to do that. I'm always looking for the smallest possible word with the broadest implication. So I do a lot with innuendo and undertone in my writing. It was hard to learn my own undertone. Take Jimmy Baldwin—and Jimmy was a friend of mine—what I loved about his essays was that he really lived and died on the dash. I didn't want to take his dash, because it was his, but I had to learn how to find my own. So I do ellipsis a lot—I put an undertone in, that gets rid of another undertone, and then shoot back in.

I think the hardest thing for me to write about has been the death of my dad. It has been difficult to the point that I haven't done it. I know that I want to write an essay about the three men in my life: my father, my grandfather, and my son. But I can't seem to get past my father. I know I'm going to do it, I'm just not ready. I want to make a statement about black men, and the ways in which I have looked at them and been affected by them. It's not as though my father and I were very close. I mean, we knew each other, he took my calls, but I was much closer to my mom. I'm told that my dad and I are very similar, so perhaps that is one of the reasons that it is hard. I think it's just the pain factor.

The two things nobody wants is their parents to die and their dog to die; the two things that you know in all likelihood will happen and that you can't prepare for. My dog had brain cancer, and I knew she was going to die, but when she did, it just hurt. I knew that my dad was going to die, but when he did it was just a lot of pain, and I was like, "Well, I can do pain tomorrow, don't really need to do that kind of pain today." I suppose that eventually it will be less painful, but I don't know. It's been ten years, but ten years really isn't that long.

The easiest thing for me to write about is my conception of the human species. I really love us, and I'm always looking at us, because human beings are such a little trip, just so much fun. I could be a fly on the wall and just laugh all day, because we are funny. We don't think of ourselves as being funny, but we are. We have these little dumb conceits. I have a dear friend who is older. She has all of her teeth, wears bifocals, but she can't hear. So I told her to pick up a hearing aid, and she says, "No, I'm not gonna get no hearin' aid, people gonna think I'm old!" And that is really very typical of people. We get into these little details that couldn't possibly matter in the scheme of things. I watch my students here at school jogging—and I love to see people jog, and I was laughing with them yesterday about Jim Fixx, because if ever there is poetic justice—Dr. Fixx dies jogging!

The thing is, and this is what I try to tell my students as writers, you don't have anything to do with your birth, so you really shouldn't have anything to do with your death. You shouldn't commit suicide, and nobody really has the need or the right to murder you, because you are going to die anyway. You don't have to do anything but live, because if you live long enough, you're going to die. So I was laughing with the kids, because I have my vegetarians, nonsmokers, nondrinkers, fitness addicts, and I think that it is great if you are trying to improve the quality of life while you are here, that's not the problem I'm having, but the end result is the same. You have to accept that. If you spend all of your time trying to defeat death, you won't get anywhere, and can't possibly enjoy living. I think that accepting this is crucial if you are going to write, because otherwise you spend your time defending against the inevitable, and that is foolish. So what I'm saying to the young writers is that you have to embrace both ends of life in order to appreciate its varieties. And if I knew how to do that effectively and permanently, I'd be on a mountain in Tibet and you people'd be trekkin' up!

What I do know is that you have to be taught to love, you have to be taught to be patient, and you have to be taught to care. The history of mankind will tell you that someone with an IQ of one or of eight billion can still be impatient and indifferent. Whatever God would be, or whatever the sparks are, when it made human beings, it put anger in, but it left out love. You have to learn to do that. I'm not dealing with Mother Theresa here, I'm talking about everyday human beings in our interpersonal relations. My students have trouble likin' the people they sleepin' with—they have lovers who they are not friendly with. Now that just doesn't make sense. So it's not so much that love isn't human nature, but that it was God or someone's little joke that says, "Here is something wonderful that you have to learn how to get!"

We should treat love like we do reading. And that would still leave us a lot of illiterate people. But we know that we can learn to read; we also know that we can learn to love. Part of that is learning self-tolerance. If we spent some time in the process called civilization, we would learn to love ourselves, and therefore appreciate differences.

I really can't say that any writers have "inspired" me, because I really hate that word. I think that we are a nation of couch potatoes who are waiting for something to compel us into doing something. So I have rejected the notion of being inspired. However, I do really *admire* the genius of Toni Morrison. You cannot like words and not just love Toni.

I met Toni when *The Bluest Eye* came out, which was truly a riveting book. I was living in New York, and she was over at Random House. So I called her up, and you know how people may tell you that you are famous, but that you really never know? Anyway, I called her secretary and said, "Hi, this is Nikki Giovanni, I wrote *Black Feeling, Black Talk*," and I was going through this whole list of books I had written to identify myself, and she said, "I know who you are Ms. Giovanni," so I felt sort of silly. Then I asked her if it would be possible to set up an appointment with Toni Morrison, and she told me she'd put Ms. Morrison on the phone. My heart started beating. We ended up having Cokes at a little place around the corner from her office, and that was just such a thrill. There's Toni, and then there's the rest of us. And I really thought that was fair to say, until Gloria Naylor came out with *Mama Day*. Naylor is quite wonderful. I think if Toni had a daughter, novelistically speaking, she would be Gloria Naylor. She really does deal with some issues, and writes exceptionally well.

I would not have any idea of how *not* to be black and a woman. Because that is a fact that will never change. What may change is whether I will continue to be a writer, or a teacher, or what I could potentially do—these are things that are not necessarily known.

But being black and a woman is known from the git go, and there's no getting around it. Black women are part of the human species, and to quote myself from my book *Gemini*, "We, black women, are the single group in the West intact, and anybody can see we're pretty shaky. We are, however (all praises), the only group that derives its identity from itself. I think it's been rather unconscious but we measure ourselves by ourselves, and I think that's a practice we can ill afford to lose. For whatever combination of events that made us turn inward, we did. And we are watching the world trying to tear us apart. I don't think it'll happen."

And I don't.

I think Terry McMillan proves that it won't. I think she's a swell young lady, and I really liked *Waiting to Exhale*. I mention her because she is the baby of the group right now, she and Tina McElroy Ansa. And I don't think you could find three black women on the face of this earth who are not happy for them, who will not cheer for them, and who don't understand that they are both part of the continuum. Not just the continuum of black women writers, but the continuum of black women. I know black women who don't read fiction who bought McMillan's book just because they wanted to support her. I think black women look to black women for validation. I think we cheer for one another. I also refer to McMillan because her novel has some shaky black women. And what makes us shaky is that we are trying to make a world for our children with very dangerous materials. But we conquer that with the fact of who we are. I've had questions about what I do, but I've never had questions about who I am. I couldn't afford to.

From

THE WOMEN AND THE MEN

Ego Tripping
(there may be a reason why)

i was born in the congo
I walked to the fertile crescent and built
   the sphinx
I designed a pyramid so tough that a star
      that only glows every one hundred years falls
      into the center giving divine perfect light
I am bad

I sat on the throne
   drinking nectar with allah
I got hot and sent an ice age to europe
   to cool my thirst
My oldest daughter is nefertiti
   the tears from my birth pains
   created the nile
I am a beautiful woman

I gazed on the forest and burned
   out the sahara desert
   with a packet of goat's meat
   and a change of clothes
I crossed it in two hours
I am a gazelle so swift
   so swift you can't catch me

For a birthday present when he was three
I gave my son hannibal an elephant
    He gave me rome for mother's day
My strength flows ever on

My son noah built new/ark and
I stood proudly at the helm
    as we sailed on a soft summer day
I turned myself into myself and was
    jesus

    men intone my loving name
    All praises All praises
I am the one who would save

I sowed diamonds in my back yard
My bowels deliver uranium
    the filings from my fingernails are
    semi-precious
    On a trip north
I caught a cold and blew
My nose giving oil to the arab world
I am so hip even my errors are correct
I sailed west to reach east and had to round off
    the earth as I went
    The hair from my head thinned and gold was laid
    across three continents

I am so perfect so divine so ethereal so surreal
I cannot be comprehended
    except by my permission
I mean . . . I . . . can fly
    like a bird in the sky . . .

NIKKI-ROSA

childhood remembrances are always a drag
if you're Black
you always remember things like living in Woodlawn
with no inside toilet
and if you become famous or something
they never talk about how happy you were to have your mother
all to yourself and
how good the water felt when you got your bath from one of those
big tubs that folk in chicago barbecue in
and somehow when you talk about home
it never gets across how much you
understood their feelings
as the whole family attended meetings about Hollydale
and even though you remember
your biographers never understand
your father's pain as he sells his stock
and another dream goes
and though you're poor it isn't poverty that
concerns you
and though they fought a lot
it isn't your father's drinking that makes any difference
but only that everybody is together and you
and your sister have happy birthdays and very good christmases
and I really hope no white person ever has cause to write about me
because they never understand Black love is Black wealth and they'll
probably talk about my hard childhood and never understand that
all the while I was quite happy

MARITA GOLDEN

MARITA GOLDEN is the author of the classic memoir *Migrations of the Heart* and the novels *A Woman's Place, Long Distance Life,* and *And Do Remember Me.* In 1993 Doubleday released an anthology edited by Marita Golden entitled *Wild Women Don't Wear No Blues: Black Women Writers on Love, Men and Sex.* Currently she is completing a novel.

Marita Golden received her B.A. in 1972 from American University and her M.S. from Columbia University in 1973. She has taught journalism at the University of Lagos, in Lagos, Nigeria, and at Emerson College in Boston. Golden has been a member of the MFA Graduate Creative Writing Program at George Mason University since 1989.

Ms. Golden is the founder and first president of the Washington, D.C.–based African American Writers' Guild. In 1990 she founded the Zora Neale/Richard Wright Award for emerging African-American college writers.

WHEN I WAS FOURTEEN my mother told me that I was going to write a book one day. Inherent in her saying that were a whole host of things. She was saying that I was smart. She was saying that I have things to say that people would want to listen to. She was saying that I am good, valuable, and worthwhile. In her saying that one sentence to me, she endowed me with so much. She wasn't just talking about writing. I know she would be very proud now.

Writing has always been an organizing tool for me, a way to confront, explain, and deal with things that I feel are very meaningful or things that I have found confusing. By the time I was in college, and I began meeting people who were actually making a living at being writers, I realized that writing might be something that could support me. Regardless of how I came to it or it to me, the actual writing has always been a kind of impulse that I simply cannot ignore. I remember while I was in college during the Black Power Movement, I was writing very militant poetry that allowed me to affirm myself as a black person in an environment that really was not quite prepared for my presence. And I don't know that I needed to prepare them. Those of us who were on college campuses in the sixties just found ourselves there, and it was often a long and painful transition process. Even now, as a professor on a white campus, I find that black students are still going through that sort of process.

The first novel I wrote was never published. It was actually a rough draft of *A Woman's Place* that I had worked on while I was living in Nigeria. I put it aside because an agent told me that I really should be writing more specifically about my experience in Nigeria. So after I did *Migrations of the Heart*, my autobiography, what I had been previously working on became, or evolved into, *A Woman's Place*. I do write somewhat autobiographically in my fiction, but not always. I think that in all fiction there is a sense of autobiography, because we tend to give our characters our own value systems, our obsessions and dreams. In terms of writing something word for word exactly the way they have occurred in my life and calling that fiction, no, that doesn't happen.

I do think that there are moments in history and in my life that have needed to go on the page and that have screamed out for fictional dramatization. For example, in *Long Distance Life*, I was writing about the civil rights movement. I felt that it was such a tremendously momentus moment in history, and the more research I did about it, the more I wanted to write about it in a fictional sense. I felt that it was almost a perfect story for a fiction writer because of all the elements involved during that time.

Fact or fiction, a story is a story and it requires imagination. There is nothing to work with until you have a story. It is a conjuring process with some autobiographical things, some things you see on the news, what you read, everything. Imagination is always the first step though, because you are imagining a character, or a story, or a response that does not exist in real life. Even though all of those things are usually inspired by real life, the one person or place or experience that you are imagining and then put on the page, is not real. Character development depends entirely on the story being told. As I live with a story, I work with the characters on a regular basis. The longer I work with the characters they simply begin to flesh out and take on a life of their own. By working with the characters, I kind of honor their spirit, and in turn, they tell me who they are. It's a very complex process. It's like baking a cake, the process is like batter, an intellectual and imaginative batter. And the final piece, the novel, or short story, or whatever, is what happens when you put the batter in the oven and it rises.

What I have observed as a teacher of fiction writing is that the best writers always come to you half-formed, almost already there. They come with a well-developed curiosity, imagination, and a sense of their right to tell stories. Those are really the best writers. They cannot be taught. But then there are people who may not have that innate gift but who have the ability to work hard. And not everybody who is a very talented writer can be a successful writer, because of the rejection one can face in the beginning. You can teach someone to write well, you cannot teach someone to be a very, very fine writer—those people really are made, born writers.

I encourage reading in my courses because it is the way to learn what a good story is, to hear how it sounds and see how it is written. And all the best writers are avid readers. And they are readers because they love the experience of being transported, which is what a good story does, and they want to learn how to do that. There is a lot of apprenticeship that goes into writing. I started out as a journalist and then moved into fiction writing, but no matter what type of writing I was doing, I was always reading like an apprentice, very critically trying to figure out how it was done.

When I started reading black women writers is when I discovered my own black femaleness. I was always reading, but not until I read Alice Walker, Audre Lorde, and Maya Angelou did I find myself in what I was reading. I could read about Anna Karenina or Emma Bovary and admire each of their stories, and be moved by it, but it wasn't my specific story. That is what was so wonderful about what black women writers did for me—they gave voice to my black female story. And that is a very big story. A very complex story. I think that even black women writers have only touched the tip of the iceberg of our story.

There isn't one way of being a black female, but I think that there are certain continuities in the black female experience. One of those continuities is, as a black woman, whether you are a middle-class light-skinned black woman, or a lower-class dark-skinned black woman, you are living in a society that really is in opposition to you, that really does not have a viable, open, accepting place for you. And you are aware of that. We see it, we always see it. Even though we have a lot of black films and black novels today, I think that in some respect, young black girls growing up today are dealing with the same things I dealt with as a black girl: "How do I define myself positively?" So that is one thing that is part and parcel with the black female experience, this sense of living in a society that has no place for you. When you are existing in the face of tremendous disbelief and doubt, you have to invent and reinvent yourself over and over again. I find that very positive and hopeful, and I feel that black women as a people are doing that.

My experience in Nigeria was really an entree into writing for me. I was there for about four years. In fact, I just went back this summer for the first time in fourteen years to take my son to see his father. When I lived there, it was a very enlightening, dramatic, compelling, contradictory, difficult, expansive experience. It was the place where I began to realize who and what I was and wasn't. I realized that I was an African-American. I changed to a comfortable place where I could be both African and American, rather than asserting one culture over the other. I came to accept the duality of who I was. I came to a kind of place where I could acknowledge and respect, and did not have to disavow, my Americanism. I came to terms with my slave ancestors, and my ancestors who may have been chiefs.

As a woman, I was made profoundly uncomfortable by many traditional aspects of African culture. That was painful, being oppressed and acknowledging the oppression. I think when I was over there, though, I was more conscious of myself racially than I was sexually. I wasn't impacted directly by a lot of that oppression against women because of my education and my mobility. When I left Nigeria, when I look back on it, I see that I had been blessed by this incredible experience. When I went, I thought that I was going to live there forever. But I began to realize that my experience there, as well as the ideals I went with, was one of several keys to open some doors. It was an experience that shaped much of my life.

When I was able to get out of Nigeria, with my son and my sanity, I sort of felt as though it was the beginning of my real storytelling. It's ironic that my professional career as a writer began with *Migrations of the Heart* instead of a novel, as I had thought it would. Coming back to the United States was sort of like coming full circle. I had left to seek family and domestic happiness, and sort of turned my back on a lot of things here in the States. I never really left America, but I felt very glad to be in Nigeria. As a twenty-seven-year-old, talented, qualified black woman, and because at that time the economy in Nigeria was very buoyant, I had a lot of opportunities. I felt like, you know, America can kiss my black ass, I'm kickin' butt over here. But having to come back to the States allowed me to finish some of those things I left, and to come full circle intellectually, emotionally, and spiritually. I carried Nigeria very heavily in me for a number of years after I came back.

To write about situations and identities that are specifically from my own personal experience is very hard. With *Migrations of the Heart*, I never thought that I would actually sit down and write an autobiography. It was difficult to write about the loss of my marriage, the loss of a certain idealism that I had when I went to Nigeria to live. The trick I used to write the book was that after a certain point, I convinced myself that I wasn't really writing about me, that I was writing about a woman named Marita Golden. That allowed me to be free to tell *her* story, not mine.

I don't know that there are really any easy things to write about though. In a sense, I guess maybe my parents are easy to write about. I think a real pivotal experience for me was the death of my parents, my mother when I was twenty-one, my father when I was twenty-two. They were very important because they really made me a writer. My mother was always very supportive of my writing talents, and when I was eighteen she got me a subscription to *The New York Times*, feeling that my interest in writing was genuine and sophisticated enough to be taken seriously. My father would always tell me stories about Sojourner Truth and Ida B. Wells and other people and aspects of black history. They both gave me a tremendous amount of confidence in myself. So that when they died back-to-back, and I wasn't aware of this until kind of recently, that loss really determined the shape of my personal and professional life to a very large degree.

In my writing, over and over again, I am trying to re-create family. And in my personal life, the whole idea of seeking family, bonds, and ties has been a pivotal one. So that very often in my fiction, like in *A Woman's Place*, the three main women characters are like a family, they are like sisters to one another. Those women and their relationships in that novel mirror the way in which I develop very intense friendships with women to supplement the loss of my parents.

In *Long Distance Life*, Naomi Johnson, the main character, is based upon and inspired by my mother. And that novel is really a meditation on family, and what family is and isn't, what it can and can't do. Because I am always seeking my parents, to affirm them, to find them, over and over again, and because ultimately, they are what family means to me. Anytime I am writing about them is when the writing comes naturally. Because putting them on the page sort of brings them back.

I think of coming through a door to my sense of self, to my black womanness, and to my writing. What I have taken with me through that door is everything that my ancestral family has given to me, my African ancestors and my diaspora ancestors. I have taken with me everything that I could hoard, everything I could salvage.

The women are picking cotton. Standing at the entrance to the village, I watch them in the field that stretches against the horizon. They work, their backs bowed beneath clouds that seem as fragile as the cotton balls filling their palms. A group of baobab trees, their trunks sunk into the reddish brown earth, limbs twisting in the shape of a half-risen sun, squat at the edge of the field. The Shona believe that even as the trees stand, timeless and elegant, they shelter spirits ready to overtake any life within reach. I've never seen a country more confident of its beauty. For this sky and these trees alone the whites must have wanted to stay. Every time I look closely at the land I know why they fought so long and so hard never to give it back to whom God gave it first. They swore, defiantly, "Never, in a thousand years." It took eighteen and now the women of this village are harvesting their own cotton, sown on plots the new black government has given them. Land sold by a farmer whose great grandfather fled an overcrowded Liverpool for the vastness of this place. And the farmer himself moved to Australia a month after the former guerrillas were elected to rule the country.

The soil is lush, productive, almost as if the years of war, the blood and bones of black and white, have enriched it. Just last month I read a report from the ministry of agriculture predicting a bumper crop of maize, wheat and cotton.

The thick wool caps that some of the women wear, red, yellow, green, dot the field with color. They undulate across the land, their bags swelling with cotton as they progress. Yet even from this distance I can see the holes and tears in their skirts and blouses. Their fat arms and broad backs, toughened by the sun, shine like polished leather. Their hair, close cropped as a man's, exposes high-cheekboned faces. How have they endured? The labor is hard, repetitive, and asks them to be as strong as mules, as uncomplaining as sheep. What is marriage, what is love faced with the long absences of husbands and men, who before majority rule worked in cities most of the women never saw, or in the diamond mines the women witnessed in nightmares. How did they honor the men's return, once a year, once every two years, to plant the seed of life in them in a cycle as faithful as that which saw the women planting maize and shucking it months later. What do they feel when receiving the once-a-month letters stuffed with a meager but welcome portion of a meager pay? How have they worked season after season land that by custom and law only men can inherit? I look again at the sky—still, yet studded with brilliant, blinding sunlight—but finding no answer there, I turn and head back into the village.

Today is my first full day in this, the last village on a tour of the rural areas for the Ministry of Women's Development. My driver, bodyguard and I arrived after dark last night, welcomed and offered a meal and a place to sleep by the chief. The circular thatched-roofed huts of the village were quiet then. As Samuel parked the Land Rover, I saw only a few children running after-dinner errands, small, shadowy figures melding phantomlike into the silence of the evening. Today is the first day I've really seen the women. But I've seen them in all the other villages and townships we've been through. I've seen the same women eking out the same type of parched, sun-dried existence. I've seen the same neglect, the same illiteracy and ignorance, for which they pay with their lives. The government says there will be change. Tells these women it will come before they die. But if it comes, it'll come for their children—children like the ones we saw a few days ago along the highway as we were entering another township. There were as many, I guess, as fifty of them sitting beneath a baobab tree watching a teacher write a math exercise on a chalkboard propped up by a chair.

It was midday and the sun was unbearable. Yet the children's sweat-drenched faces followed each move of the chalk across the blackboard. And I'll always remember the sight of slender brown arms thrust into the air, fingers squirming in excitement as the teacher pointed to a boy who rose, shirtless, barefoot, in shorts tied at the waist by string, to give an answer that earned him applause from the children around him. Maybe the change will come in time for them. Maybe the promise, this time, won't be broken.

I've seen the same women and children in other villages but I know that these women and children are different. And as the women troop back into the village for lunch and rest, I see the evidence of war on their bodies. I see the woman who wears an eye patch, the young girl who hobbles on a maimed foot. These people spent a good part of the war in a guerrilla-controlled resettlement camp on the border with Zambia. Several months before the end of the fighting, the camp was raided by government soldiers. That day in the capital, the guerrilla leaders, representatives of the British and the Americans, and officials of the minority government met in a wood-paneled hall in Parliament House to continue their months-long efforts to negotiate peace. And at that moment fifteen hundred miles away, white soldiers who had painted their hands and faces black attacked the camp, killing most of the soldiers protecting it, in a surprise burst of fire from M-16s. The civilians were rounded up from tending small gardens, from cooking and from rest.

When the women saw the guns aimed at them, I imagine that some must've dropped to their knees in prayer. The babies on their backs, smelling the fear inside the beads of sweat on their mothers' necks and inhaling it, began crying as when first expelled from the womb. The soldiers pursued those who ran, smashing dead bodies with armored cars. Rifle butts knocked the women unconscious, knives slit their breasts, slashed their throats, and of the men there—mostly old and feeble—they cut off penises, arms and legs. Babies were smashed against the hoods of jeeps bought from the U.S. by South Africa and sent as an act of friendship to the minority government. And many of the women wondered, as soldiers grabbed them and prepared to kill them, wondered in the seconds they had left, gazing at the skin around the eyes that was not blackened, and at the thin lips twitching with hate, wondered why the gods of the whites had abandoned them. Why they had nothing more than death to believe in and fear. Three hundred people were killed that morning. When it was over, only the endless cries of a few toddlers crawling among the corpses, their fingers digging into the dusty, dry earth, filled the air.

Those who escaped hid in the bush, where some died of their wounds. Those who survived ate worms and lizards, drank their own urine.

The camp sat odorous and defeated for three days before the guerrillas returned from their own raid and helped the survivors bury the dead. After the independence agreement was signed, the people who survived the massacre left the camp and began planting cotton on the former estate of Jonathan Leeds, now quite prosperously resettled in Sydney, Australia.

Nearly forty women sit before me, their bare calloused feet covered with dust. A few wear sneakers without laces or shower thongs worn down to the edge on one side. The toddlers and babies held in their arms wriggle restlessly, struggling for freedom. The older children, having finished a lunch of mealie-mealie scooped out of tin bowls with fingers or thick hunks of bread, chase one another raucously in the distance, wrestling and dancing in circles, their laughter and taunts a kind of music.

Samuel, the driver, sits outside the hut he and Renson, my body-guard, share, a transistor radio held tightly to his ear. And even in his khaki uniform he still manages to look like a hipster. It must be the sunglasses, I think, imagining his eyes closed tight behind them as his head bobs in time with the sound of Bob Marley's "Crazy Baldhead" drifting in spurts over to where the women and I sit.

The chief of the village walks toward us, his generous paunch appearing to precede him on its own. He's tall, a broadly built man without the hungry, tattered look of his people. In fact, he resembles nothing so much as a civil servant, dressed in a short-sleeved white shirt and trousers. Before the war there were over one thousand people in this village. There are five hundred now, almost three quarters of them women. As the chief nears us, the women shift in anticipation, shush older children, offer squalling babies a breast to suck, try vainly once more to smooth the wrinkles in their clothes and rivet their eyes on the chief. Wiping his face with a cloth and stuffing it into his pants pocket, the chief first greets the women as a group. They respond in a humble, reverent chorus. He tells them the purpose of my visit and commands them to listen to me. When he has finished, I don't tell the women that the ministry has sent me to evaluate and assess their status. And based upon what I've seen, to write a report that will be given to the prime minister to hopefully strengthen his commitment beyond rhetoric to women's rights. I tell them simply that I have come not to talk, but to listen.

So unused are they to telling others what they want that they sit before me in response to my request, whispering among themselves and eyeing me like one of their sex who might just possibly be mad.

Finally near the front a young woman stands up. "We need water nearby," she says timidly, stopping to look at the chief and at the other women for approval to continue. "We still trek for many miles bringing water from the streams." Her voice, which had trembled in an unsure whisper at first, steadies itself. The hands she had hidden behind her back become eloquent punctuations to her words, traveling over the heads of the other women, all turning away from me to her. "We need electricity, like there is in the larger townships. Our children need a school so they do not have to read under the hot sun." The other women are now stirring, murmuring in agreement, sitting straighter and marshaling their own sense of denial. "It has been two years since we won back our land," the woman charges. "We have seen no changes. Where is the revolution? When will it come to us?"

Another woman, fat, bulging, her arms and legs broad as tree stumps, hoists herself up onto her feet. Small rivers of sweat slide down her dark, fleshy face. She yanks a soiled scarf from her head and wipes her neck, pointing, as she does, to the young girl beside her on the ground, one of the girl's legs cut off at the knee, a pink and brown stump of dry dead skin and flesh. "My daughter has not seen a doctor in months. Her leg is swelling and our treatments have not healed it," she charges. The girl, whom I saw hobbling around the village on crutches, lets her head drop like a beaten animal beneath her mother's pitying glance. "Why is it only the soldiers and the 'comrades' are seen by doctors? She lost her leg carrying maize to soldiers hiding in the bush. My daughter was a soldier too. We in this place have wounds. Wounds that have not healed in all this time." The other women shake their heads, erupt into a chorus of aahhhs and uh-huhs that bear witness to the woman and her child. The woman lowers herself, landing heavily on the ground beside her daughter, whom she pulls with one of her strong arms closer, pressing the girl's head onto her shoulder.

"What of the roads?" someone shouts, eager and testy. "Promises were made. Promises must be kept." The words are ominous and plaintive and instantly overtaken, hoisted into the air as broad as a banner, as the women break into a clamorous outcry of complaint. The bruised, never enough, relentless nature of their lives seems to strike them all at once. Suddenly the chief stands, his jowls bunched in amazement. Too harshly, he silences them, warning them to retreat into a humility they will never wear comfortably again.

"What of a bride price?" I ask when they are quiet. "The ministry wants to abolish it." A wave of laughter travels among them. And from the rear there is a shout, "There are so few men we fear many of us will never again have the need for bride price. We fear our daughters will not know it either. But bride price must be paid or the ancestors will make babies die in the womb and the marriage cannot survive. The ancestors will inflict the penalty on generations that follow." The women in the ministry have made stamping out the bride price and the remnants of polygamy a top priority. But they meet their stiffest resistance from women such as these. Women who with their children bore the brunt of the war and were not counted officially among the dead. Women who after all the years of fighting now want tradition and peace, men again, children and bride price. "You are like all the government people who tell us what we should want and don't listen to what we need," the first woman who had spoken says in exasperation. "Bring the revolution to us. That is all we ask."

JUNE JORDAN

JUNE JORDAN was raised in the Bedford-Stuyvesant neighborhood in Brooklyn, New York. She is the author of twenty-one books, including the award-winning novel *His Own Where*, chosen by *The New York Times* as one of the Outstanding Books of the Year in 1971 and a finalist for the National Book Award. Her poems, articles, essays, and reviews have appeared in various publications.

Ms. Jordan has worked in film, city planning, theater, and has taught at several colleges and universities. For eleven years she was professor of English at SUNY at Stony Brook, where she also served as director of the poetry center and the creative writing program. Currently, Ms. Jordan is professor of African-American studies at the University of California at Berkeley, where she is establishing a new, campus-wide program—"Poetry for the People." Her most recent publications are *Technical Difficulties: African American Notes on the State of the Union*, Vintage, 1994, and *Haruko/Love Poems*, new and selected love poetry, Serpent's Tail/High Risk, 1994.

I GOT INTO LANGUAGE as a little girl for many different reasons. I started reading when I was around two years old. My father made me read a lot of things that I couldn't understand the meaning of, but I could hear the words, and the music they made, and I liked that a lot. My father would tell me to read Paul Laurence Dunbar as well as Shakespeare, without saying this is a black poem and this is a white poem—he just told me to read them by the next day. At that point, Elizabethan English was about as alien to my ears as turn-of-the-century Paul Laurence Dunbar's so-called dialect. So I became aware early on about the variations of language.

Both of my parents were West Indian immigrants. They also raised one of my cousins, who is about four years older than I, and she was a really good mimic. When company came to visit, she and the rest of the family would imitate people. We would imitate West Indians, people from the South, all kinds of people. It was just something that we did, and we all thought it was hilarious and also very interesting to imitate the way other people talk, including ourselves. So that of course also made me real sensitive to the differences in the spoken language. Delightful differences. My family in its own divided way was also very religious. So that meant studying the Bible, going to church, and hearing the Scripture. On the one hand, this meant repetitive exposure to narrative of that sort. And then it was about just hearing the Scripture, which, in terms of syntax and grammar, is pretty well put together—it's good writing of a kind.

And then there was the language of the street. I was born in Harlem, but I grew up in Bedford Stuyvesant, which is also an all-black community as well as Harlem. A lot depended upon style—you could say whatever you wanted, but if you said it the wrong way, you were a dead duck. I realized then the impact of language style. Then, when I was about six years old, my aunt and her husband moved into the top floor of a brownstone in Brooklyn. Her husband was my Uncle Teddy, and he spoke Black English. He was an incredible storyteller, and jivemaster, and he adored words and wordplay. His Black English was impeccable, and I worshiped the ground he walked on. Nobody could talk the way he could talk. So I studied him. Those are the reasons I got into language. The reason I stayed in language was because it became my business.

I made money writing poems for my classmates. I would write poetry on demand—you know, if someone had a crush on somebody, or wanted to break up with somebody, or what have you. Depending on the length, and how difficult it would be for me to get into it, you know, I had a sliding scale. I made pocket money that way. Writing or poetry never seemed like an oddball thing for me to get into, or a particularly solitary thing. It has always been, in my head, an emphatically social act, because it has a purpose that involves other people. It had to work for other people, not just for me. And at that time, it had to work for my classmates because my business depended on it—if they didn't like it, they wouldn't come back. I never received any encouragement from my parents to write poetry.

In grade school, I got encouragement from my teachers to write, but that was just school. Writing was my homework. Later, when I got to prep school, I started taking writing more seriously and, in fact, became intoxicated with words. Just recently I received an award from my prep school, Northfield Mt. Herman, and my classmates were telling me about a term paper I had done for biology on tissue culture written completely in iambic pentameter—so I know I had to have been intoxicated with words to do that. I don't really remember doing that paper, but my class-mates did. So writing was something that became part of my basic identity. Obviously the biology teacher probably would have pre-ferred to have the paper written in prose, and I didn't really care, cause that wasn't the way I was going to write it. I couldn't have done the paper at all if I had had to write it in prose, it wouldn't have been interesting to me. After prep school, when I went to Barnard, we had survey English courses, and it was real hard for me to sit through those courses, and my professors allowed me to write something of my own that met the craft requirements of the period we were discussing. So by the time I left Barnard, my craft and knowledge as a writer were rather elaborate and solid.

After I got married and had a child, I started writing a poem called "Fragments from a Parable." The goal of that long poem was to claim, to really wrestle my own language out of an enemy language. I felt at that time that English was completely the language of my enemy. This was coincident with my own Black Nationalist period—politically and culturally. I wanted to see what I could do, because no other language was gonna work for me in this country except some kind of English. So I worked on this poem for about eleven years. And at the end of writing it, I felt I could work with English and not feel that I was in some way participating in my own suicide. I still feel that English is the lan-guage of my enemy, and it is difficult, for sure, to work with it. Especially with poetry, because poetry requires a lot of precision. It's very hard trying to be precise using lexical items that somebody else has loaded with a lot of garbage. So much of it is garbage. And by that I mean flat out lying, with pathological con-notations that are indefensible, historically indefensible, intellectu-ally indefensible. It's difficult. And poetry is about telling the truth. So the hardest thing you can try to do is to take the currency of language that is made available to us and try to individuate it so that it really conveys what you mean, or feel, or see, or know. That's pretty hard. But that's the task of a poet. I think of the political essays I write as a game. Essay writing is not about telling the truth. It's about putting together an argument so that you can persuade somebody to think a certain way. I think of it as a technical undertaking . . . a technical difficulty.

I've met a whole lot of poets throughout my life, and a whole lot of them don't tell the truth, and I didn't know that in the beginning. Joy Harjo is one of my best friends and favorite poets, but sometimes she makes her stuff up! She's one of the leading Native American poets in the country. And I didn't know she wasn't telling the truth! There's one poem of hers called "Santa Fe," and I've never been to Santa Fe, but after reading this poem, I was like, "Jesus Christ, I've gotta go there," right? So then I meet a few people who had been to different parts of the country including Santa Fe, and I asked them, "Do they have lilacs on their motorcycles there?" And these people looked at me like I was crazy! And now I don't even think I want to go, because I have to choose between the poem and the actual city, and it sounds to me like the city is not gonna make it. So she doesn't view poetry in the same way I do, which is of course fine.

I think Adrienne Rich tells the truth in her poetry, to the best of her ability. I'm not sure that the truth is a concern for her in the same way it is for me, but I do think it is one of her criteria. The young black poet Cornelius Eady is hilarious, and he tells the truth—I'm crazy about his stuff. And a bunch of black poets from earlier on were telling the truth—Ntozake Shange, Thulani Davis, Quincy Troupe, Sonia Sanchez—all at different times I think were telling the truth through their poetry. Each in their own way, I think they used poetry to name the universe in their own image, as well as to identify their own struggles with language and power and liberation. So I would say, out of the whole civil rights movement, as well as the movement for freedom as women, in both instances, there were a lot of poets who, out of necessity, used language as a necessary route to the truth—to saying "I'm here."

When I write essays I always try to keep in my mind a hypothetical adversary I am trying to convert into an ally or a comrade. I write essays to galvanize my folks, whoever they are, to go and kill somebody, you know, something like that. I don't really have an audience in mind when I write poetry. I just write what it is and hope to the extent that I succeed that I will be able to make a profound connection with a lot of different kinds of people. I hope anyway. So that in some way, people who feel connected to what I write are spoken for. And that does happen—someone will come up to me after a reading and say, "I've felt that way," or "I was completely with you when you said that." I find that very gratifying. I don't want to speak for other people, I would not presume to do that, but in trying to say what I think, and assuming that I am a pretty ordinary person when it gets down to rock bottom, I hope I will be able to make a connection through language that other people will be able to use for themselves, ordinary or otherwise. Usually when I write an essay, I have to fax it someplace right away. I am most times relieved to be finished with it, and don't really care if I see it again anytime soon, because I know I will. Writing an essay is like looking back on a fight that's still going on. I think, "Did I cover this?" "That's an interesting statistic that I should have included," "Did I address that person?" It's kind of like having a fight with someone, walking away to take a break, but knowing that I'll be back—like the break was to run through my head all the information, covering all the bases and making sure I didn't leave myself open.

When I write a poem, there's no fighting. I am seeking the right word and searching for the best way to say something—the funniest, the most harrowing, something in that superlative realm. I can usually tell when I'm not satisfied with a poem, because I will leave it on the pad, and I won't show it to anybody. And I'll worry about words. I worry about whether I gave a poem all the possible craft advantages I could, I worry about whether it is as tight as it can be. But when I do feel satisfied with a poem, I need immediate feedback. I'll call one of my friends, and my phone bill is outrageous, and say, "Can I read you something?" And of course if they don't drop dead on the floor after hearing it, I'm miserable. I think, "Oh Christ, I've got more work to do, this ain't over."

I'm not concerned about missing anybody with my writing. I think that there is a racist, patronizing point of view around understanding certain ideas where black folks are concerned that I do not embrace. Most everything I write, I test out. Big audiences. Live. And that's poetry as well as essays. So it's not too hypothetical to me whether it's gonna hit or not. If it hits, I know. If it doesn't hit, I know. For example, my essay "Requiem for a Champ," which is an essay about Mike Tyson. Well, that's about as crafted an essay as I've written. I had to write an extremely, extremely calculated essay, very carefully put together, 'cause that stuff is hot. I remember thinking, "Oh, June, don't even touch this," but that's why I had to touch it. It's really amazing to me that everywhere I've read that essay, all these different kinds of black men have come up to me afterward and given me a hug. When I say all different kinds of black men I mean middle-age guys as well as really young men. And it's great, because that means to me that they got it, that they were listening. It is a very tricky argument to put out there, but they got it. Because yes, what Mike Tyson did was awful, totally monstrous, yes, but where'd he learn that? The whole idea of indicting him instead of the society that created him is ridiculous to me

I make observations in my writing that will lead to action. I make suggestions for action. I observe that in any university, the football coach earns far more than the chancellor, let alone the social counselor, or the psychology counselor, or the professor teaching humanities. This type of injustice is really not intractable. And I suggest that we can do something about it. We can say to the football coach, "Yo, no, you can earn a little less than $600,000 a year, so we could hire some good soul to work with someone like Mike Tyson for say, $50,000 a year, you know? I think you can make $550,000." This is a practical suggestion. So I would go back and not say "indict society," because that is tired language, but find ways to get the point across in a very tangible way.

A pivotal event for me as a writer and a poet happened during the sixties. It was a great big poetry reading down in Jackson, Mississippi. It was all black women poets—Sonia Sanchez, Audre Lorde, Mari Evans, I mean, you know, everybody at that time. It was held in a huge auditorium. I just thought I was the baaaadest poet in the world with my baaaad Brooklyn self. I got down there and was blown away. The place was packed, and folks was all dressed up, families and children and deacons. And all my poetry had profanity in it, and I was like, "Oh shit, I can't read anything!" And Sonia said, "See? I told you so!" I mean, it was like church. Everybody was on time—in black Mississippi folks was on time! And I would never have presumed to imagine that being a poet merited that sort of respect. And trust. At that moment, I realized that as a black writer, people were looking to us/to me for vision, leadership, and most of all, people were looking to us/to me for The Word.

I think as long as you try to be clear, and I always try to be clear, people will get it. I may have a word in my writing that somebody may not know, but that's just a word, and that's it. I think mostly my language is extremely straightforward, and I have worked on it quite a bit. It is not academic. And it is not common. You'll never see the word *feminist* in my work, or *patriarchal*, or any of that—I just don't use words like that. I'm not writing for the academy. I don't give a shit about the academy. I'm writing for people who read. Mainly I try to reach college students, which is a huge, heterogeneous, and important audience to reach. Academic language includes a lot of stupid words. I don't even like to use the word *racist*. If I do use it, I have to really try and use it in a way that is still fresh, so it still hits and stings, so that people under-stand that "I'm here to *kill* you because of this." You know what I mean? I'm not saying, "Well that was a racist incident," no, I don't mean it was a racist incident, no, I mean, "I'm gonna *kill* you cause that was racist!" How you rest that word in any usage, to give it the power that it originally had, is important. For example, in the context of Rodney King, some people call that a racist episode, which makes the word *racist* sound tepid—you know, it was pleasant, unpleasant, racist, casual, and so on. All those words sound the same. I try to use words, whether in prose or poetry, that people can understand, that make them feel in an intense way. I'm a writer, that's what I do.

Generally I don't read fiction, because to me, it's about making stuff up. I mean, I don't think I really have time, because I'm trying to figure out what's going on in the world. It's very interest-ing to me that all of my friends who write fiction are multimillion-aires. Sometimes I think I might write some fiction to make some money, but I don't think it'll ever happen. Some people write fiction and some people don't. I have done it, and feel like I accomplished it well. It was a love story that I wrote entirely in

Black English, because I wanted to show that Black English is not just jive nonsense.

Fiction is so weird to me, but also fascinating—you really can make something up just because you feel like it. I think some people do it really well and make a great contribution to literature. I know that Toni Morrison and Alice Walker do a lot of research before they write, and so there is a sense of reality in their work. Their work is really well crafted. Toni is fabulous and *awesomely* literate. So for her to make a commitment to fiction writing is really something to me. I think a lot of the things that she has created in her work are really beautiful. And Alice too. I seem to have sort of a strange attitude towards fiction I guess. I don't think there's a lot of time. Life is too short not to tell the truth.

Mike Tyson comes from Brooklyn. And so do I. Where he grew up was about a twenty-minute bus ride from my house. I always thought his neighborhood looked like a war zone. It reminded me of Berlin—immediately after World War II. I had never seen Berlin except for black-and-white photos in *Life* magazine, but that was bad enough: Rubble. Barren. Blasted. Everywhere you turned your eyes recoiled from the jagged edges of an office building or a cathedral, shattered, or the tops of apartment houses torn off, and nothing alive even intimated, anywhere. I used to think, "This is what it means to fight and really win or really lose. War means you hurt somebody, or something, until there's nothing soft or sensible left."

For sure I never had a boyfriend who came out of Mike Tyson's territory. Yes, I enjoyed my share of tough guys and/or gang members who walked and talked and fought and loved in quintessential Brooklyn ways: cool, tough, and deadly serious. But there was a code as rigid and as romantic as anything that ever made the pages of traditional English literature. A guy would beat up another guy or, if appropriate, he'd kill him. But a guy talked different to a girl. A guy made other guys clean up their language around "his girl." A guy brought ribbons and candies and earrings and tulips to a girl. He took care of her. He walked her home. And if he got serious about that girl, and even if she was only twelve years old, then she became his "lady." And woe betide any other guy stupid enough to disrespect that particular young black female.

But none of the boys—none of the young men—none of the young Black male inhabitants of my universe and my heart ever came from Mike Tyson's streets or avenues. We didn't live someplace fancy or middle-class, but at least there were ten-cent gardens, front and back, and coin Laundromats, and grocery stores, and soda parlors, and barber shops, and Holy Roller churchfronts, and chicken shacks, and dry cleaners, and bars-and-grills, and a takeout Chinese restaurant, and all of that usable detail that does not survive a war. That kind of seasonal green turf and daily-life supporting pattern of establishments to meet your needs did not exist inside the gelid urban cemetery where Mike Tyson learned what he thought he needed to know.

I remember when the City of New York decided to construct a senior housing project there, in the childhood world of former heavyweight boxing champion Mike Tyson. I remember wondering, "Where in the hell will those old people have to go in order to find food? And how will they get there?"

I'm talking godforsaken. And much of living in Brooklyn was like that. But then it might rain or it might snow and, for example, I could look at the rain forcing forsythia into bloom or watch how snowflakes can tease bare tree limbs into temporary blossoms of snow dissolving into diadems of sunlight. And what did Mike Tyson ever see besides brick walls and garbage in the gutter and disintegrating concrete steps and boarded-up windows and broken car parts blocking the sidewalk and men, bitter, with their hands in their pockets, and women, bitter, with their heads down and their eyes almost closed?

In his neighborhood, where could you buy ribbons for a girl, or tulips?

Mike Tyson comes from Brooklyn. And so do I. In the big picture of America, I never had much going for me. And he had less. I only learned, last year, that I can stop whatever violence starts with me. I only learned, last year, that love is infinitely more interesting, and more exciting, and more powerful, than really winning or really losing a fight. I only learned, last year, that all war leads to death and that all love leads you away from death. I am more than twice Mike Tyson's age. And I'm not stupid. Or slow. But I'm Black. And I come from Brooklyn. And I grew up fighting. And I grew up and I got out of Brooklyn because I got pretty good at fighting. And winning. Or else, intimidating my would-be adversaries with my fists, my feet, and my mouth. And I never wanted to fight. I never wanted anybody to hit me. And I never wanted to hit anybody. But the bell would ring at the end of another dumb day in school and I'd head out with dread and a nervous sweat because I knew some jackass more or less my age and more or less my height would be waiting for me because she or he had nothing better to do than to wait for me and hope to kick my butt or tear up my books or break my pencils or pull hair out of my head.

This is the meaning of poverty: when you have nothing better to do than to hate somebody who, just exactly like yourself, has nothing better to do than to pick on you instead of trying to figure out how come there's nothing better to do. How come there's no gym/no swimming pool/no dirt track/no soccer field/no ice-skating rink/no bike/no bike path/no tennis courts/no language arts workshop/no computer science center/no band practice/no choir rehearsal/no music lessons/no basketball or baseball team? How come neither one of you has his or her own room in a house where you can hang out and dance and make out or get on the telephone or eat and drink up everything in the kitchen that can move? How come nobody on your block and nobody in your class has any of these things?

JUNE JORDAN

I'm Black. Mike Tyson is Black. And neither one of us was ever supposed to win anything more than a fight between the two of us. And if you check out the mass-media material on "us," and if you check out the emergency-room reports on "us," you might well believe we're losing the fight to be more than our enemies have decreed. Our enemies would deprive us of everything except each other: hungry and furious and drug-addicted and rejected and ever convinced we can never be beautiful or right or true or different from the beggarly monsters our enemies envision and insist upon, and how should we then stand, Black man and Black woman, face-to-face?

Way back when I was born, Richard Wright had just published *Native Son* and, thereby, introduced white America to the monstrous product of its racist hatred.

Poverty does not beautify. Poverty does not teach generosity or allow for sucker attributes of tenderness and restraint. In white America, hatred of Blackfolks has imposed horrible poverty upon us.

And so, back in the thirties, Richard Wright's Native Son, Bigger Thomas, did what he thought he had to do: he hideously murdered a white woman and he viciously murdered his Black girlfriend in what he conceived as self-defense. He did not perceive any options to these psychopathic, horrifying deeds. I do not believe he, Bigger Thomas, had any other choices open to him. Not to him, he who was meant to die like the rat he, Bigger Thomas, cornered and smashed to death in his mother's beggarly clean space.

I never thought Bigger Thomas was okay. I never thought he should skate back into my, or anyone's, community. But I did and I do think he is my brother. The choices available to us dehumanize.

And any single one of us, Black in this white country, we may be defeated, we may become dehumanized, by the monstrous hatred arrayed against us and our needy dreams.

And so I write this requiem for Mike Tyson: international celebrity, millionaire, former heavyweight boxing champion of the world, a big-time winner, a big-time loser, an African-American male in his twenties, and, now, a convicted rapist.

Do I believe he is guilty of rape?

Yes I do.

And what would I propose as appropriate punishment?

Whatever will force him to fear the justice of exact retribution, and whatever will force him, for the rest of his damned life, to regret and to detest the fact that he defiled, he subjugated, and he wounded somebody helpless to his power.

And do I therefore rejoice in the jury's finding?

I do not.

Well, would I like to see Mike Tyson a free man again?

He was never free!

And I do not excuse or condone or forget or minimize or forgive the crime of his violation of the young Black woman he raped!

But did anybody ever tell Mike Tyson that you talk different to a girl? Where would he learn that? Would he learn that from U.S. Senator Ted Kennedy? Or from hotshot/scot-free movie director Roman Polanski? Or from rap recording star Ice Cube? Or from Ronald Reagan and the Grenada escapade? Or from George Bush in Panama? Or from George Bush and Colin Powell in the Persian Gulf? Or from the military hero flyboys who returned from bombing the shit out of civilian cities in Iraq and then said, laughing and proud, on international TV: "All I need, now, is a woman"? Or from the hundreds of thousands of American football fans? Or from the millions of Americans who would, if they could, pay sur-realistic amounts of money just to witness, up close, somebody like Mike Tyson beat the brains out of somebody?

And what could which university teach Mike Tyson about the difference between violence and love? Is there any citadel of higher education in the country that does not pay its football coach at least three times as much as the chancellor and six times as much as its professors and ten times as much as its social and psychological counselors?

In this America where Mike Tyson and I live together and bit-terly, bitterly, apart, I say he became what he felt. He felt the stigma of a priori hatred and intentional poverty. He was given the choice of violence or violence: the violence of defeat or the vio-lence of victory. Who would pay him to rehabilitate inner-city housing or to refurbish a bridge? Who would pay him what to study the facts of our collective history? Who would pay him what to plant and nurture the trees of a forest? And who will write and who will play the songs that tell a guy like Mike Tyson how to talk to a girl?

What was America willing to love about Mike Tyson? Or any Black man? Or any man's man?

Tyson's neighborhood and my own have become the same no-win battleground. And he has fallen there. And I do not rejoice. I do not.

GLORIA NAYLOR

GLORIA NAYLOR graduated from Brooklyn College and received an M.A. from Yale University in Afro-American Studies. She is the author of the internationally acclaimed quartet of novels: *The Women of Brewster Place*, *Linden Hills*, *Mama Day*, and *Bailey's Cafe*. In April 1994, the stage adaptation of *Bailey's Cafe* premiered at the Hartford Stage Company.

Balancing her commitments as a writer and her work as president of One Way Productions, the independent entertainment production company she began in 1990, Ms. Naylor has participated in Robert Redford's Sundance Institute and is currently in pre-production on *Mama Day*, the feature film adaptation of her third novel.

As her novels now mark their twelfth language translation, Ms. Naylor maintains a hectic international schedule of speaking engagements while also finding time to research her next novel. Ms. Naylor currently resides in Brooklyn, New York.

WHEN I WAS COMPLETING *The Women of Brewster Place*, I hoped that I would have a quartet of novels. I set that as a goal for myself. Once I had done that quartet, then that would be the foundation for my career.

In *Brewster Place*, I mention Kiswana Brown from *Linden Hills*, in *Linden Hills*, I mention the character Mama Day, and in *Mama Day*, I mention *Bailey's Cafe*. The mention of these characters and places in each book is not just in passing, they were all meant to be loosely connected. These four books were to say: "Gloria, you are now a writer." So *Bailey's Cafe* was very special to me when it came out last year, because it was the end of the quartet.

My books are like children, each child brings something special to their home, and to their parents, each child is loved, and sometimes loved for different reasons. It works that way with my characters when I look over these last twelve years. I am particularly close to my older female characters, I have lots of fun with old women. And the children characters, too.

What I do to ground myself in each place I am writing about is to put myself there, and to then say to myself I guess the same things I say to my writing students: "What is going on in this room, what are the intangibles that are happening? What does the air feel like, smell like, how does this table feel, the texture of it under my hand?" That's something that just comes naturally to me because I am literally there. I have gone to that place.

I remember in *Linden Hills* how difficult it was to write what I used to call "the downstairs sections," because it was cold in that cellar room, and the woman who was locked down there was scared. Fear smells a certain way on the human body—it's not pleasant, it tastes like nickel in the mouth. To be with that woman in that room, and to smell her fear and to be cold with her, it was very depressing. I inundate myself that much in the environments that I write about.

What I attempt to do, how I see myself, once I've been allowed into these environments, is to be a chronicler of what's going on around me. With *Mama Day*, I traveled to the Sea Islands. I am from southern parents, so I grew up in a very southern home right here in New York City. I knew the foods, I knew the speech patterns, I knew the behavioral codes of the South, because that was my enculturation. But I did not know the Sea Islands, per se. So I had to go. I went to do what I call "tactile research." I went to just walk the terra firma, to smell the air, to see those trees. It helped with the book because it made me understand that history is tangible in that part of the country. Not only just the people— the people talk about the Civil War as if it happened last week— but you have live oaks there that were already a hundred years old when the Civil War took place. That kind of thing. So I do that kind of research. New York is where I was born, so writing about New York is writing about what I know. All of the other locales in my work have been metaphysical, so they exist nowhere. They are presented as emotional situations.

I have my own criteria and patterns of belief. I happen to believe that there are people who can take you, or even take their own minds, to other planes. I believe in psychics. There are dimensions that we are not privy to, those of us who use what we're told is about 10 percent of the capacity of our brain. In *Mama Day* when Mama Day was at the "Other Place" with Bernice, I personally believe that indeed something did happen on another plane—but it is written so the reader can take it on any level they wish. I was pleased that the book did not become didactic, or that my own beliefs influenced what the reader could take out of it, and that it worked on the different levels I wanted it to work on.

Some people have read *Mama Day*, and have said, "Well, Mama Day just relaxed Bernice, she was playing psychological tricks on her." And we do know that when some women have no physical reasons barring them from conception, there are indeed emotional reasons. The first thing that any specialist will tell them is to just relax and forget about it. So it can be read on the level that Mama Day was just simply playing games with Bernice, psychological games—with the pumpkin seeds, and giving her the right foods. If you look at those foods, I took them straight out of a textbook. Those are foods that build up the blood, and foods that are meant to relax you—the yeast in the things she had to eat, and the B complex vitamins are good for nerves. So Mama Day was treating Bernice homeopathically. But at that final step, in the "Other Place," did they go somewhere else, did something else happen? That's down to you and your own beliefs.

Mama Day is a very strong woman, and the values that she lives by she got through the powers of her African Ancestresses. I think that the "strong black woman" stereotype in this country flattens the livelihood of black women. While there may have been in our collective history, our own individual histories, times that we have had to be strong, or times that we have had to be sensual, and you can go on down the line—nurturing, earth mothers—that is only one tiny aspect of everything that is going on in an individual or in a collective historical reality. The stereotypes about black women exist for the same reason that stereotypes exist about any group—it is a way of boxing in human beings, it is a lazy way of thinking about people. It bars us from the uncomfortable feeling that having to accept complexity gives us in the western world.

As a black woman myself, I have grown up with certain strengths. I also happened to have been very fortunate to have grown up with relatively healthy parents who endowed their daughters with a sense of self, and a sense that our achievements can be limitless as long as we don't limit ourselves. They knew that if we had looked to the outside world for affirmation, we would have had none. At *best* we would have had none, at worst we would have had the stereotypes, and the things that would have held us down, if not tore us down. I feel stronger than some of my white female counterparts because of the nurturing that needed to be done, the steel that had to be put into my backbone just for me to exist at all in any kind of healthy way.

Being a black woman also means that I have to try harder, and get less for the effort. At times that bothers me, when I think that the payback is so small for the kind of effort I am expending. I have to work past not just someone else's natural reticence, but I have to work past all the blocks they have put up in their minds about my color and my gender. As a black woman *writer*, I tend to just not be overly concerned with the white world. I'm what you might call a Cultural Nationalist, in the sense that I feel that within my own community and sphere, there is a wealth of material. What motivates me, what I find most interesting, is writing about the dynamics of human beings within those particular worlds. We are people of color, and if you took a family portrait, we would just be gorgeous. And we would range.

Cocoa, from *Mama Day*, is a very different black woman from me. What I never had that Cocoa has is the sense of her own history. She knows, back to almost the trip over, who her antecedents were. Her family never moved. Cocoa also has a problem with the lightness of her complexion that I never had. She grew up a pariah in a community that glorified dark skin, and found dark skin lovely. Irrespective of her light skin, George describes her—"your fists balled up on your hips, you drawing blood with your never-ending mouth—you were, in spirit at least, as black as they come." And that spirit and pride came from a tangible proof of her lineage and ancestry.

When I think about our collective ancestry and history, as a race, I realize that it is those unnamed individuals who were strong. There were a lot who came here and weren't, and those people are not around—the physically weak, or the emotionally or psychologically weak. Our history was an experience that would have done most people in, and it did, depending on what statistics you look at. It's just the minority who survived. So now that means, if we subscribe to Darwin, that we who did indeed survive are carrying some damn good genes.

Black men are in my work mostly to stand as counterparts to black women, which makes them vital. I do think, although I haven't always felt this way, that it is harder for black men in this society to survive. Given the fact that this is a patriarchal society, I think that they expect more of themselves than women do. The ways that black men are given by this society to define themselves as men entail that they succeed in a way that women are not expected to. Failure resonates differently for black men. Although I consider myself a feminist, I think on some level we as women say to ourselves, Yeah, but I'm a woman. I never understood why men would go to the wall for some issue. I thought, what's the point, let it go, what's the problem? But I see now that it is in the socialization of men. To have these expectations floating in the universe, and then to be a black man, and not be able to reach those expectations—it resonates differently.

I didn't realize that black women wrote until I was about twenty-seven years old. That's when I discovered Toni Morrison's *The Bluest Eye.* Then I went on to read Zora Neale Hurston, and Paule Marshall, and Ntozake Shange, who had a huge influence on me. *For Colored Girls . . .* had just hit Broadway, and there was the choreo-poem itself that had been published, and I loved that. The idea that someone said: "Y'know what? It hurts to be a black woman, and I'm gonna tell you all the reasons why it hurts." I thought that was so courageous and real.

I try not to create for myself glorious stereotypes for who and what I am. In the sixties, we were *all* "black and proud," and therefore everything black was good. I think there was a need for the pendulum to swing that way because it had stayed in the other direction for so long. But I like the fact that perhaps now we are coming back to the middle ground, and saying that we are human beings.

There is a rock, and I was terrible at earth science when I was a kid, but there is a certain kind of quartz that when you break it open there are all kinds of colors in it, depending on how you turn it in the light. I have lived, in my forty-three years, several distinct lives. I would liken myself to that rock because it is a rock that is formed by fire, and when you break it open there are all these different edges and colors. And they are all strong.

From
MAMA DAY

While things are going on loud like that inside the beauty parlor or in front of the general store, other things are moving along quietly. And they can be the more important. See, we ain't paid too much attention to the change in Bernice Duvall. She's a lot less nervous than she used to be, and she's walking everywhere now. That old green Chevy stays parked in her side yard and she makes it the three miles from the south end to the stores at the bridge junction on foot. She's there once a week to pick up her special order of blackstrap molasses, brown rice, and brewer's yeast. She'll stand a while and exchange the time of day with folks, her packages hoisted up on them hips that are starting to fill out slowly but surely. And if someone asks her about her mother-in-law, she don't get that funny little twitch around her mouth anymore. She'll say real pleasant that she's helping Pearl make her dress for the wedding— Pearl is gonna be Ruby's matron of honor—and things are going along just fine. The only time Bernice will hurry along is when she's got frozen meat in her bag: twice a month the store brings in a box of liver, beef kidneys, and beef heart for her. Nobody asks why she and Ambush is eating them strange things now, and Bernice don't offer the information. But she'll nod her head and agree out loud when for the hundredth time someone says they'll be glad come spring. Her words hold a different ring, though—it's like when the visiting choir sings they'll be glad going on to glory come Judgment Day. Contentment is the last thing folks want around here in the winter, and so Bernice Duvall goes unnoticed as she quietly moves about the business of preparing for her miracle.

Down the road at the Days' there's busy preparation for a miracle that Miranda says has already happened: Cocoa's marriage. She was beginning to think that she'd never live to see the day, and she'd geared herself up to live for a long time. It's still kinda hard to believe that telephone call that came from New Orleans, but she'd spoken to the boy herself and they got the pictures in the mail this month. He had a strong face, and a good strong name—George. He was gonna need all the strength he could get to put up with Baby Girl, Miranda thinks. Just out-and-out aggravating, that's what she could be—demanding to have herself a double-ring quilt as a wedding present. Like all folks got to do this winter is sit around sewing together tiny bits of cloth till their fingers ache. Not a bit of consideration for her arthritis or her grandma's failing eyesight. And she knew they weren't gonna let anyone else help, not for something like this. All the chalking, padding, stretching, and hemming was up to them if it was gonna be done at all. And you couldn't send an old poor-mouth quilt with one double ring, no—from edges to center the patterns had to twine around each other. It would serve her right if it took till next year, and it probably would if they had the sense not to keep at it all day and a good part of the night.

"Well, that's it for me. It's after ten o'clock." Abigail bites off the knotted end of her thread. She sighs and runs her hand along her end of the quilting frame. "It may be taking forever, but it's gonna be some kind of beautiful. You were right, Miranda, using that cambric muslin instead of a regular cotton lining is gonna make this feel like velvet. But it's a pain in the neck to sew—a stitch will slip away before you know it."

"Just gotta keep waxing your needle."

"Next to threading, I think I hate waxing the most."

"I hate the whole mess. This cutting, shaping, measuring. And I told Baby Girl, don't ask me for spit after this."

"But she did finally say she'd settle for a simple pattern."

" 'Cause she ain't got no pride. This'll be passed on to my great-grandnieces and nephews when it's time for them to marry. And since I won't be around to defend myself, I don't want them thinking I was a lazy old somebody who couldn't make a decent double-ring quilt."

"Great-grands." Abigail shakes her head. "It couldna been more than yesterday when I was a bride. And now we're sitting here talking about my great-grandchildren." Abigail's eyes look off in the distance, pride and sadness all mixed up in one.

"No, we're sitting here *planning* your great-grandchildren." Miranda licks her thumb to thread another needle. "You can't count on nothing with these young people today. And knowing my grandniece like I do, if she ain't found herself a saint, it's gonna be a long haul between that honeymoon and her getting me that new teacup with Great-Great Aunt on it."

"Miranda, you're always downing Baby Girl. If this doesn't work out, why it gotta be her fault? We don't know nothing about him."

"He told us all about himself on the phone."

"His name? What he does for a living? And a whole lot of promises anybody can make. Talk is cheap, Miranda."

"I know, that's why I listened real careful to the way he talked. Remember what he said when you told him to take good care of her? He said, 'She has all I have.' "

"Yeah, real pretty. But how many right here in Willow Springs done heard them same words? Junior Lee probably said it to Frances, and you see where Frances is."

"No, Abigail—listen to him good now. The boy ain't said, 'All I have is hers.' We both know that's a lot of nonsense, 'cause nobody would—or could—give away *all* of themselves to somebody else. That person is an out-and-out liar, or if they was of that mind, they wouldn't be nobody worth living with. No, he said—'She has all I have.' That means sharing. If he got a nickel, she's got a part in it. He got a dream, he's gonna take her along. If he got a life, Abigail, he's saying that life can open itself up for her. You can't ask no more than that from a man."

"Maybe you're right." Abigail stands up and stretches her back. "Like you was right about this muslin. But I'm going to bed now. How much longer you sitting at this?"

"Just a bit more. It's less I'll have to do tomorrow."

"Don't forget to cut off my lights."

"Woman, don't I always cut off your lights?"

"No, 'cause you're getting senile like me."

The old walnut clock in Abigail's living room ticks away as Miranda's silver needle slips through the layers of padded cloth: the curve of each ring is fixed into place by sending the needle down to the bottom and up. Down and up, a stitch at a time. She's almost knee deep in bags of colored rags, sorted together by shades. The rings lay on a solid backing of cotton flannel; from a distance it looks like she's bending over a patch of sand at the bottom of the bluff when it's caught the first rays of a spring moon—an evening cream. The overlapping circles start out as golds on the edge and melt into oranges, reds, blues, greens, and then back to golds for the middle of the quilt. A bit of her daddy's Sunday shirt is matched with Abigail's lace slip, the collar from Hope's graduation dress, the palm of Grace's baptismal gloves. Trunks and boxes from the other place gave up enough for twenty quilts: corduroy from her uncles, broadcloth from her great-uncles. Her needle fastens the satin trim of Peace's receiving blanket to Cocoa's baby jumper to a pocket from her own gardening apron. Golds into oranges into reds into blues . . . She concentrates on the tiny stitches as the clock ticks away. The front of Mother's gingham shirtwaist—it would go right nice into the curve between these two little patches of apricot toweling, but Abigail would have a fit. Maybe she won't remember. And maybe the sun won't come up tomorrow, either. I'll just use a sliver, no longer than the joint of my thumb. Put a little piece of her in here somewhere.

The gingham is almost dry rot and don't cut well, the threads fraying under her scissors. She tries and tries again just for a sliver. Too precious to lose, have to back it with something. Rummaging through the oranges, she digs up a piece of faded homespun, no larger than the palm of her hand and still tight and sturdy. Now, this is real old. Much older than the gingham. Coulda been part of anything, but only a woman would wear this color. The homespun is wrapped over and basted along the edges of the gingham. She can shape the curve she needs now. Extra slow, extra careful with this one: she pushes the needle through, tugs the thread up, two ticks of the clock. Pushes the needle through, tugs the thread down two ticks of the clock. *She ain't bringing that boy home mid-August.* Miranda feels a chill move through the center of her chest. She doesn't want to know, so she pushes the needle through and tugs the thread down, tugs the thread up. *Or the next August, either.* She tries to put her mind somewhere else, but she only has the homespun, the gingham, and the silver flashing of her needle. *Or the next.* It doesn't help to listen to the clock, 'cause it's only telling her what she knew about the homespun all along. The woman who wore it broke a man's heart. Candle Walk night. What really happened between her great-grandmother and Bascombe Wade? How many—if any—of them seven sons were his? But the last boy to show up in their family was no mystery; he had cherished another woman who could not find peace. Ophelia. It was too late to take it out of the quilt, and it didn't matter no way. Could she take herself out? Could she take out Abigail? Could she take 'em all out and start again? With what? Miranda finishes the curve and runs her hands along the stitching. When it's done right you can't tell where one ring ends and the other begins. It's like they ain't been sewn at all, they grew up out of nowhere. She'd finish off this circle with the apricot toweling, leave the two openings to connect in some of that light red crepe, and call it a night. This quilt was gonna be treated real tender, and it was gonna cover a lot of tenderness up there in New York on them cold winter evenings. But she won't bring that boy home mid-August. Be a long time before Willow Springs sees him.

She turns off the lamps before she leaves for home. She wasn't gonna work on that quilt by herself no more at night. When Abigail, stopped, she'd stop. If it took 'em longer, so be it. Some things you don't need to know, especially when you can't do nothing about it. The past was gone, just as gone as it could be. And only God could change the future. That leaves the rest of us with today, and we mess that up enough as it is. Leave things be, let 'em go their natural course. The night air hits her face, it's sharp and chill, but she can feel the earth softening under her feet. Spring's coming. Wild azaleas be blooming soon, the thorn apples and crepe myrtle. Them woods won't look the same. No fertilizer, no pruning—no nothing, and they'll beat her flowers blooming by three weeks. Yes, spring was coming. And would God forgive her for Bernice? But she wasn't changing the natural course of nothing, she couldn't if she tried. Just using what's there. And couldn't be nothing wrong in helping Bernice to believe that there's something more than there is. It's an old house with a big garden, and it done seen its share of pain. And I'm just an old woman who'll be waiting in a rocking chair . . .

The first new moon come spring. She can hear her coming, smell her coming, long before she makes that turn down by the old pine stump. Moving through the bush, guided by the starlight that glints off the two pair of eyes waiting and rocking, both unblinking. One pair cradled low in the lap of the other, soft rumbles vibrating its feathered throat. One pair humming a music born before words as they rock and stroke, forefinger and thumb, gently following the path of feathers, throat, breast, and sides. The right hand stroking, the left hand cupping underneath the tiny egg hole that sucks itself open and closed, open and closed. Two pair of eyes breathing as one when hope rounds that bend. She can taste the fear that hesitates on the edge of the garden walk; it's thick in the air moving before the feet passing by the tuberoses, the camellias, the hanging vines of the dwarf honeysuckle. Feet passing into the other place where flowers can be made to sing and trees to fly. Fear trembling at the bottom of the porch steps, watching the gleaming of two pair of eyes, hearing the creak of wood against wood under the soft rumbling from feathers, the humming begun in eternity. But it's hope that finds a voice: Mama—Mama Day?

The right hand strokes, the left hand reaches out, the palm wet from the cradled egg, gray and warm. Confusion waits a bit too long. The shell dries and grows cold under the hidden moon. One pair of eyes unblinking, one pair frowns and smashes the egg into the porch steps. Silent, she pleads for another chance. But she must wait—and listen. Not to the humming, not to the creak of wood against wood. Naw: the moon inching toward the horizon, the tiny hole sucking itself open and closed, open and closed. The left hand reaches back out. Knowing takes the egg while the shell's still pulsing and wet, breaks it, and eats.

Now, it only takes a nod of the head to move them all inside. Pine chips smoking on the fire blazing in the parlor hearth makes the air steamy and sweet. Every shadow in the unlit room is dancing along the floor and walls. She ain't gotta be told why the dining table is covered in a white sheet and has padded boards nailed upright on one end. She strips down naked, rests her head on the embroidered pillow, and props her feet high up into the scooped top of each board. It'll be easier if she closes her eyes. In the morning she can tell herself it was all a dream. And it can't be human hands no way, making her body feel like this.

Nine openings. She breathes through two, hears through two, eats through one, the two below her waist, and two for the life she longs to nurse. Nine openings melting into the uncountable, 'cause the touch is light, light. Spreading each tiny pore on each inch of skin. If she could scream, she would, as the touching begins deeper at the points of her fingertips to expand the pores that let in air, caressing down the bones of each finger joint to the ones that join the palm, the wrist, the lower arms. Her shoulders, sides, and stomach made into something more liquid than water, her breasts and hips flowing up against the pull of the earth. She ain't flesh, she's a center between the thighs spreading wide to take in . . . the touch of feathers. Space to space. Ancient fingers keeping each in line. The uncountable, the unthinkable, is one opening. Pulsing and alive—wet—the egg moves from one space to the other. A rhythm older than woman draws it in and holds it tight.

BARBARA NEELY

BARBARA NEELY is a novelist and short-story writer whose short stories have appeared in numerous anthologies including: *Things That Divide Us, Speaking for Ourselves, Test-Tube Women, Constellations, Angels of Power, Street Talk, World of Fiction,* and *Breaking Ice.* Neely's first novel, *Blanche on the Lam* (St. Martin's Press, 1993), won the Go On Girl! award for best debut novel, and the Agatha, the Macavity, and the Anthony for best first mystery. She is also the recipient of a 1994 Women of Conviction Award for arts and literature from the Massachusetts section of the National Council of Negro Women. The second Blanche White novel will be published by St. Martin's Press in 1994. Neely is at work on a third novel and a one-act play.

Also a feminist activist, Neely is the cochair of the Board of Women for Economic Justice and a founding member of Women of Color for Reproductive Freedom. She received the 1991 Community Works Social Action Award for Leadership and Activism for Women's Rights and Economic Justice.

I WAS DOWN at the corner of Market Street and California Street in San Francisco where there was a typical California Street band playing—a white guy on guitar, a black guy on saxophone, a Chinese woman on drums, one of every nationality they could find, and there was a semicircle of tourists standing around listening to the band. This one black woman approached the semicircle. She was very short, very thin, with very dark skin, patent leather hair, polyester print slacks, and a strange ill-fitting shirt from who knows where, and she started dancing. Of course people started cracking up. They thought it was hilarious. The woman altered her dance pattern and began going around the circle, pointing her finger at different people, making very serious eye contact. It got very quiet. When she got to me, I swear I could hear this woman's voice saying to me, "If you wanna dance darlin', you better do it today." I went back home and tried to write that woman's story. I have boxes in my basement. I never finished it, but once I launched on that project, I had to have something from then on. And now, writing is my addiction. I have to have it.

It has taken me a long time to satiate that addiction. I think I reached a point where I didn't have any other choice but to write. I used to write short stories for friends' birthdays when I didn't have any money, but never took myself seriously as a writer. The idea of being a fiction writer, which was the only kind of writer I was ever interested in being, was not a way to help your mother pay her real estate taxes. I also didn't really believe I had anything to say. There is a kind of self-revelation that you do when you write fiction, regardless of whether or not you are personally in the story—I think I was too vulnerable to put myself out there until maybe my early thirties. By that time, I decided that I wanted to write, but it didn't occur to me when I applied to the Ph.D.

program at the University of Michigan to apply in literature. I did the same thing with the Ph.D. that I did with my master's degree—"What degree will I be able to make a living with?" And after I left the school, I felt like such a fool, because I realized that Gayl Jones was teaching there, which sort of compounded the error of not going into the literature program. I went into architecture and urban planning, and dropped out—could not kiss that much ass in *nobody's* semester.

In my first meeting with my advisor, he sat there with a list of professors and checked off the names of those whose ass I needed to kiss on a daily basis. I thought it was wonderful of him to do that for me, but it became clear to me shortly thereafter that I wasn't going to make it through. So considering myself as a writer has come fairly recent, perhaps in the last four years or so, even though I've been publishing short stories since 1980. I had always considered myself to be a social activist who wrote, or the director of so and so who writes. The writing has always been on the side. It's only been in the last few years that I've allowed myself to move writing into the center and identify myself primarily as a writer.

When I began writing *Blanche on the Lam*, my first novel, is when that identity as writer consummated. The character of Blanche initially came from a woman I knew in North Carolina who had a look that inspired me to create a heroine in her memory. I can't remember exactly how I made the decision that Blanche would be a domestic worker. I knew I wanted her to be representative of who black women are, presently and historically. Both of my grandmothers did domestic work, so I heard plenty of stories about the triflin' white folk they would work for. I also had a friend who had a middle-class education and a middle-class job who decided of her own free will to give up her middle class job to do domestic work because she wanted to work for herself. So I knew that it was not out of the realm that there were people out there who do domestic work by choice. And I respect that decision. Blanche is really about a lot of things. She is an interesting woman, she fascinates me. We share some attitudes, she and I. We are both childless by choice—that is, we have no biological children.

I always knew that I never wanted children. There are certain kinds of sacrifices that I'm just not interested in making. I must say that it is partly because of my own view of how child rearing needs to be done, and how the focus of your life needs to be when you are helping this creature evolve into a decent human being. To me, there is no more creative work than that. There is no more difficult work than that. I knew that I would not be able to do it the way I knew it needed to be done. Why take it on? It's like taking on race car driving if you are afraid of speed—why take it on? I didn't think I could put into child rearing what I thought ought to be put into it. It's not that I didn't think I had the capacity. I didn't want to make the sacrifice.

I came out of a very wild, extended family. On my street when I was growing up, I had aunts, cousins, uncles, and a grandmother, all within a block. I think there are children who recognize the disadvantages of childhood at an early age. I was one of those children. I've never cared for authority in any form whatsoever. My mother was a very young mother, and while I had four or five other mothers on my street, because she was young and because I was arrogant, I always felt like, Well, she doesn't know a great deal more than me, how come she gets to make all the decisions? So in that sense, I was not a happy child. But I was a happy child in the sense that among all of these relatives on the street, there were no other girlchildren, making me very sought after.

Some of my earliest memories are of when my mother and

father had split up, and my mother had moved to Philadelphia. I remember my cousin coming down on the train when he was on leave from the army, putting me inside of his bomber jacket, and taking me to his house to spend the weekend with him and his wife. One of the reasons that memory sticks with me now is that, here were these people—a man on leave from a life-threatening situation home with his wife for whatever amount of time, and what they see as a good time is having me for the weekend? It really does put things into perspective and make you realize how special you can be to someone's life.

There's also a story in my family about my great-aunt, who once plopped my naked infant body down in the middle of the Thanksgiving dinner table as the centerpiece. So in that sense, it was always very nurturing. But in terms of friends, there were very few black people in my town, I was the only black child in my school from third grade until I graduated from high school. And there is a kind of pain in that experience that you can't even explain to people. My mother has asked me now why I didn't tell her. The only thing I can think of is that crazy thing that children always do, and that is if there is something wrong with a situation then you assume that you are somehow responsible for it. So to go to her and tell her about it was in fact to say, "Here is this awful thing that I have somehow created." And that would hurt.

When I was coming of age, somebody else was defining what it was to be a black woman. And that somebody was telling me that I needed to keep my mouth shut and walk two steps behind so that black men could come into their ascendency, and that when the revolution was won, the boys would bring me along too. My mother didn't really raise any stupid children. It became very clear to me very quickly that this bit wasn't gonna go. I grew up in a family of very strong women. At our family reunions, it is very clear where the center is. There has never been any question in these women's minds, or in my mind, who holds families and societies together. And all the family stories are about the women. Men get mentioned incidentally, or there will be a picture with the story of a man and a wife, and the person showing the picture will say, "That's Uncle Harry, and he was so and so, and this is Aunt Evelyn, let me *tell* you about her. . . ." So there is a way in which I accepted all of that strength, but at the same time there was the message from the larger society, from men that is, to keep my mouth shut and my legs open.

When I got into the political arena, I identified myself first by my race. In the process of being politically active, I understood that that wasn't enough. I understood that there was this other part of my identity that was also political and was not accepted, and that that part of my identity was being a woman. I was not prepared to make any sacrifices. I was not prepared to be a good girl, I was not prepared to be faithful to any male, I was not prepared to be spoken to as though I was a fool, I was not prepared to look up to people who were fools. . . . I was not prepared to do any of the things that women essentially have to do to manipulate men, or to have a traditional relationship in this society. Once I ran into that wall, I knew that I had to alter my definition of who I was. I had to understand that while my strength as a black woman is unique, if I turned into a white woman today, my butt would still be kicked. I have to be just as true to my womanness as I am to my blackness. The thing is, of course, that when I came to that decision, I realized that there is no conflict there, because my womanness is the womanness of a black person. I can honor both in the same way by operating with personal integrity. By talking back I honor both.

I was lucky with my own personal relationship in that I met a man who made me understand that there were ways in which men can be moved from where they are—from their fear of women's power, from their fear of not feeling powerful, from their belief that the way you run a family is by making the most money, from their belief that a woman's job is to pick up their socks and do all that sort of strange stuff. I met this guy who made me understand that with a man who is ready to change, and with the right training, you can help a man develop himself into a full human being. I think that men are socialized not to be human beings. Women aren't necessarily socialized to be human beings, we are simply more in touch with what makes human beings human—and that is our emotions.

When I met this man and realized that there was hope, I also realized that there are men who are secure enough, nonthreatened enough, and intelligent enough to recognize their own best interest. That is, it is in their best interest to be with a woman who is strong and forthright, who is going to call you on your stuff, and be called on, who will hold you when you cry, and who will allow you to hold her when she cries—that there is nothing more exhilarating than a reciprocal relationship. I got lucky enough to find someone who was at a point in his life where he was willing to accept that. And so then we had four or five years of struggle building a foundation. Now, we understand and respect each other, and I can say that this person is a dear, dear, true friend . . . who calls me on my sexist language! But it is work. And it is tiresome. You know, saying week after week, "You cannot leave here until we both get it straight," and I admit that I am more prone to just leave. I'm likely to just throw up my arms and say I'm taking a walk, and he says, "Yeah? Well what if you get hit by a car?!" So we still have to discipline ourselves. One of the difficulties in getting that kind of disciplined relationship is that you have to put out, you have to own all your tacky stuff, you have to admit when you're wrong, and you have got to not use any of the manipulative techniques that we've all learned to use. And it is hard. But I tell you, it is the most sustaining thing in my life. It amazes me. And the man is beautiful in every conceivable way.

I feel a close connection to black people as I write about the experiences we have as black women. And the black women writers I know are integral to my writing. Hattie Gossett is extremely important to my life. I talk to Hattie regularly. She is a very good sister and a fine writer. I use the black women writers I know personally, as well as the ones I don't know, as sort of touchstones for when I get scared of doing it, or when I feel like I'm not going to be able to do it. I think Toni Morrison is arguably the best writer in the English language, probably in the universe. There is writing, such as Morrison's, that makes me want to write. Not because I think that I can write as well, or that I can write the same thing, but because it is such a wonderful example of what writing does. She writes books that you can read out loud and want to read over and over. Morrison always immediately makes me want to get to my desk. The special thing that she did for me was to make it clear to me that there was room in literature for stories about the kinds of people who I wanted to write about and who I cared about.

Morrison is like this huge umbrella out in space under which there is all of this space for the rest of us. I always think of her as our/black people's psychiatrist. There is a way in which she reveals us to ourselves as human beings that is just amazing. I've always said that probably our major difficulty in this country as black people is not what is happening to us externally, but what is and is not happening to us internally, beginning with a serious emotional exploration of slavery and what it has meant in reference to our perception of the world—the ways in which we raise our children, the way we manage our relationships, all of that. There is this huge and festering sore within all of us that we won't even get near, let alone feel. And then comes *Beloved*. *Beloved* for me was definitely a catalyst to start me thinking about ways to deal with that pain.

When I don't write, I'm not well. And sometimes it is a way to talk about painful subjects both with some distance and maybe not objectivity, but a kind of universality. Like taking your little pain and making it big enough for other people to recognize their pain in there somewhere, or something like that. I use writing as a way of describing what's under that rock. I try to take my own experience and sort of transmogrify it. Right now with the sequel to *Blanche on the Lam*, I'm having to reconstruct Blanche's relationship history—all the relationships she's had with men since she was nine years old.

What I first did was to look at my own relationship history as a way of trying to think about what a relationship history looks like. I learned that it isn't linear, that I can't very often make a connection between why I had a relationship with this sort of person and then the next relationship was with someone whose personality was really far-out. I began to think about the ways in which I was attracted to people, the different reasons I was attracted to each person, and how it was not always the same with each relationship. Then I look at Blanche's personality and think, "Where would her people be? Where would the men in her life be?" So I think I do take some of my own stuff and integrate it with my characters. In fact I know I do. I had an incident with a cab driver in North Carolina who beat me up because I talked back to him. Within a year after that, I wrote a short story about a woman whose son returns from prison after having committed a rape, and her response to that. I know that that story grew out of the experience I had with the cab driver. So it's like finding the pain and using it.

I don't have a lot of romanticism about the publishing world. I don't have a lot of false respect for people I have to work with in the publishing world. I have lived a life, there isn't much you can run that I haven't heard before. I don't expect to make a trillion dollars writing. I do it because I love it. And that means doing it my way.

Usually, Blanche hated waiting on table and being treated like just another utensil. But this evening she was disappointed when Grace told her she needn't stand duty in the dining room. She was curious about this guest. She couldn't recall exactly what Everett had said about him at lunch, but it had revolved around the lie that Emmeline had the flu and something taking only ten minutes. She'd looked him over as closely as she'd dared when Grace rang for more rolls. At least she'd learned his name, Archibald. He looked like a Hollywood version of a southern gentleman: snow-white hair, glowing pink skin, and the kind of face people she'd worked for called Roman. Blanche understood this to mean a high forehead, a big nose, and no lips to speak of. While she was in the room, conversation either stopped or was nicey-nice talk.

After dinner, she carried the coffee tray into the sitting room, a small, bright room, across the hall from the living room, done in yellow and lime-green wallpaper with chair cushions to match. An open liquor cabinet stood against the far wall. The furniture was white, with curved and carved arms and legs. Everett and his guest stood by the window. They were deep in conversation that only they could hear. Grace wasn't there and neither was Mumsfield. Blanche began pouring their coffee, but Everett dismissed her with a flip of his wrist.

"When Nate, who looks after the garden and grounds, arrives," Grace told her, "we'll be going up to Aunt Emmeline's room. We'll need you both." Grace's face was slightly flushed. "There's something I, that is, my husband and I . . . It will only take a mo . . ."

A soft sound came from the back door, something between a knock and scratching. Blanche opened it to a short, wiry old man whose skin reminded her of some deep red-black wood polished to a high sheen. He was clutching a grungy baseball cap and bobbing and weaving like a punchdrunk fighter. His denim overalls were faded to a watery blue. He gave Blanche a brief nod and slipped by her into the kitchen. She recognized him as the person she'd seen in the garden. Now she watched him bow and scrape and "Miz Grace" all around the kitchen until the object of his ass-kissing led them up to the back stairs. If it's a put-on, he ought to be in the movies, Blanche thought. If it's for real, it's pitiful.

On the way upstairs, Grace kept up a constant trickle of questions and comments about the garden and the weather and the ducks on the pond. She and Nate laughed together over little remarks that meant nothing to Blanche. She did notice that Grace was wringing her hands as though she were hoping to get gold out of them. The hollow laughter of a TV laugh track seeped from beneath a bedroom door that Blanche bet was Mumsfield's.

The smell of cheap liquor and cigarettes had been replaced in Emmeline's room by the pungent fragrance of eucalyptus. A humidifier sent a jet of mist into the overheated room. Emmeline was hiked up on a mass of creamy white pillows edged with pink embroidered roses. Her blue satin bed jacket was trimmed with white lace. A matching cap covered her Little Orphan Annie Afro. Her eyes were red-rimmed but keen. She observed her visitors from over a linen handkerchief she held to her nose and mouth.

"Why, Miz Em, it sure is good to see you!" Nate performed a kind of jerky bow as he moved beyond the foot of the bed until he was near Emmeline's side. Blanche hung back, watching from just inside the door.

"I sure am sorry to see you feeling sss . . . sss . . . so . . ." Nate stuttered and stumbled through telling Emmeline how sorry he was that she was ill. Emmeline clutched her handkerchief closer to her face and seemed to shrink further into her pillows. She flashed her eyes at Grace. Grace opened her mouth and reached out her hand to Nate, but whatever she intended was forestalled by a knock on the door. Everett ushered Archibald into the room.

"Cousin Archibald." Emmeline spoke in a high, sweet whisper that was very different from the bitchy whiskey rasp Blanche had heard earlier.

Archibald crossed the room to the far side of the bed and set his briefcase on the table by the window. He took the hand Emmeline held out to him.

"Cousin." He bowed low over Emmeline's hand. His silver hair gleamed in the light from the window. "You can't know how much it means to me that you asked to see me, personally, after so long. I . . ."

Emmeline lowered her handkerchief and coughed a quick succession of loud barks in Archibald's direction. He flinched and took a quick step back from the bed. "Don't try to talk, my dear."

Emmeline coughed again. Archibald snatched his own handkerchief from his breast pocket and brought it quickly to his mouth and nose. After a few moments, his eyes widened and crimson crept up to his forehead. He looked quickly down at Emmeline, who was once again hidden behind her handkerchief. By the time he shifted his gaze to see if Grace and Everett had noticed, he had already stuffed the offending handkerchief back in its proper place. Blanche saw laughter in Emmeline's eyes.

Archibald opened his briefcase. The minute she saw that sheath of heavy, thick, clothlike paper, Blanche knew they were there about money. Archibald fussed with his papers while Everett fetched the rolling tray from the other side of the room. He pushed it to the bed so that it extended across Emmeline's lap.

"I really do hate to bother you, Cousin, but you did insist that I come today." Archibald laid the papers on the tray in front of Emmeline. "If you'll just sign here." He used his pen as a pointer.

Emmeline lowered her handkerchief and produced a series of loud, dry coughs. This time, Emmeline wasn't the only cougher. Blanche had to manufacture a cough of her own to cover the grin that sprang unbidden to her face when Archibald practically threw the pen on the tray and jumped away from the bed as though his life depended upon putting distance between himself and his cousin.

Blanche was now positive Emmeline was making mischief. She tried to catch Nate's eye, to see if he'd noticed it, too, but he had eyes only for the baseball cap he was squeezing to death between both hands.

Emmeline was reading through the four or five sheets of paper Archibald had given her. She ran her eyes down each page in a leisurely fashion, then picked it up and turned it face down on the tray with slow, deliberate movements before going on to the next page. Every once in a while she coughed into the handkerchief she still held to her mouth. Warning shots, Blanche thought. The air in the room was as charged as a thunderstorm.

"It's a wise change, if I may say so." Archibald cleared his throat. "All the other items, of course, remain the same." Archibald moved a tad closer to his cousin. His eyes seemed to implore her not to infect him any more than she'd already done. "The bequests to the servants, the generous gift to the Daughters of the Confederacy . . ."

He petered out as the old lady continued to read, or at least pretended to read.

Grace was breathing through her mouth in short, quick bursts. Her hands were white-knuckled fists at her side. Everett lay his hand on the small of Grace's back for just a moment. She gave him a poor excuse for a smile, but Everett never took his eyes off Emmeline.

There was a light coating of sweat on Everett's forehead. And Blanche could almost feel Nate concentrating on the baseball cap in his hands. Did Emmeline's teasing Archibald account for all the tension bunched in the room? Blanche doubted it.

"Of course, I agree with you," Archibald said, as though responding to something Emmeline had said. "Mumsfield's a fine lad, a clever boy . . . all things considered. But managing an estate as large as yours is a complicated business. Better to have older, more . . . er . . . ah . . . capable members of the family in charge of his affairs." He smiled over at Everett and Grace.

"The firm is at your service," he told them. "And, of course, I personally will be glad to—"

He was cut off by a hacking cough from Emmeline. He stepped back until his butt bumped against his briefcase on the table behind him. Emmeline snatched up the pen and signed the last page, coughing as she wrote. Blanche felt rather than heard a collective sigh from Grace and Everett. Archibald looked a little shocked. Was it the old lady's quickness with the pen that surprised him?

He grabbed the will before Emmeline could cough on it again. He held it gingerly, as though it were one of those smallpox blankets the early settlers gave to the Indians. Blanche half expected him to whip out a pair of rubber gloves. He laid the last page on the table beside his briefcase and motioned Blanche and Nate closer. He handed the pen to Blanche and pointed to a line beneath Emmeline's signature. Blanche wished she'd said she couldn't write. But at least it didn't sound as though Mumsfield was being cut out of his money, only having it handled by his cousins. Blanche wrote her name in a round, girlish hand on the line next to Archibald's manicured pink-white finger. It occurred to her that just because Mumsfield's cousins were handling his money was no reason to assume his money was safe. Archibald took the pen from her and handed it to Nate. Nate leaned stiffly over the table and signed his name in shaky script.

"I'd like to stay and chat, Cousin, but I can see that you need your rest." Archibald stuffed the pen and the will in his briefcase and moved quickly toward the door. Emmeline coughed again, as if to hurry him along. Everett followed him out of the room.

Grace dismissed Nate with a nod and a vague smile, and told Blanche that Everett would lock up. Nate followed Blanche down the back stairs.

"What do you make of all that?" Blanche asked him.

"I sure wisht I wasn't in it." His eyes looked older than dirt. His shoulders drooped. "You ain't from round here, is you?" He gave Blanche a searching look that took in her hair, and her feet, and all in between. Including, she thought, some parts that don't show.

"Farleigh," she told him. "But I been living in New York for a while."

"Figures. You talk like city. Fillin' in for them Toms who works for 'em in town, hunh?"

Blanche nodded. "What about you?"

"I been working for this family since Miz Em was a girl. Come here to work when I was twelve years old. So was Miz Em. We got the same birthday, ya know." Nate hooked his thumbs in the straps of his overalls. "I worked for her daddy and her daddy's daddy. Outlived both them suckers." Nate chortled a vicious little laugh and headed for the back door. "I was looking forward to going to Miz Em's funeral, too," he added. "But now . . ."

"Why you say that? She ain't dead yet, and neither are you."

Nate hesitated. "Miz Grace is one of them kinda people always worried about her standin' in the community—that's how she puts it, like she was some kinda church or the government or something. That's how I know it's got to be him that's behind this mess."

"What mess? You mean the new will?"

Nate went on talking, but he didn't answer Blanche's questions. "I never thought he was much. Course, he thinks plenty of hisself. Hardest work the man does is brushin' back his hair. Unless you call gamblin' and runnin' after women 'work.' He's kinda like a pet Miss Grace bought to show off to her friends. To prove she could get her a man, too, I guess, even though he *is* a hand-me-down, so to speak." Nate rubbed his jaw. The sound of his whiskers rasping against his hand sounded like shifting sand.

"Maybe I made a mistake," he said. "Maybe I was wrong 'bout him bein' too lazy to cause any harm 'cept to run through Miz Grace's money quick fast and in a hurry. Or so they say."

"I still don't understand," Blanche told him.

Nate opened the back door, then turned to look at her. His eyes called her to attention. "You don't need to understand," he told her. "I wisht I didn't." He put on his baseball cap. "You look after yourself, Miz City." He tipped his cap in her direction and went quickly out the door.

Blanche followed him and called softly to him to come back. Nate waved to her over his shoulder, shook his head from side to side, and kept on going. Blanche could tell from the way he shook his head that it was useless to run after him. He was through talking to her for the night. Tears of disappointment sprang to her eyes. She hadn't realized how tightly she'd latched on to him, the only black person she'd been with since she'd left home for the courthouse. Once she'd gotten a glimpse of who he really was, she wanted to ask him how it was that Mumsfield didn't know about Emmeline's alcoholism, what it was that made Grace so nervous, and why had he changed into a statue in Emmeline's room. But he was gone, and she was standing there being a meal for the mosquitoes. She swatted at one buzzing near her ear.

The night wrapped itself lovingly around her limbs. Some long-locked door creaked open almost wide enough for her to see inside, to remember how it was she knew the night so well and felt so very comfortable in it. With her moment of near-remembrance came a sense of personal worth, of strength, and fearlessness that buoyed her. She was distracted from her memory by a sharp bite on her ankle. But the feeling roused by her almost-recollection was so sweet she couldn't let it go. She turned out the kitchen light and sat down on the back stoop.

The stars were bright and silver-blue. The moon was a child's drawing, lopsided, bright, and full of magic. Blanche stretched out her arms and let her head fall back. She could feel muscles pulling in her forearms and tightening at the back of her neck. She relaxed against the step and stared out into the deeper dark that hung above the garden and in the pinewoods beyond.

Night Girl. She hadn't thought about her private game for years.

Cousin Murphy was responsible for Blanche's becoming Night Girl, when Cousin Murphy found eight-year-old Blanche crying because some kids had teased her about being so black.

" 'Course they tease you!" Cousin Murphy had told Blanche. She'd leaned over the crouching child as she spoke. Blanche could still smell her Midnight Blue perfume and see her breasts hanging long and lean from her tall, thin frame.

"Them kids is just as jealous of you as they can be! That's why they tease you," Cousin Murphy had told her. "They jealous 'cause you got the night in you. Some people got night in 'em, some got morning, others, like me and your mama, got dusk. But it's only them that's got night can become invisible. People what got night in 'em can step into the dark and poof—disappear! Go any old where they want. Do anything. Ride them stars up there, like as not. Shoot, girl, no wonder them kids teasing you. I'm a grown woman and I'm jealous, too!"

Cousin Murphy's explanation hadn't stopped kids from calling her Ink Spot and Tar Baby. But Aunt Murphy and Night Girl gave Blanche a sense of herself as special, as wondrous, and as powerful, all because of the part of her so many people despised, a part of her that she'd always known was directly connected to the heart of who she was.

It was then that she'd become Night Girl, slipping out of the house late at night to roam around her neighborhood unseen. She'd sometimes stop beside an overgrown azalea by a rickety front porch and learn from deep, earnest voices of neighborhood deaths and fights, wages gambled away, about-to-be-imprisoned sons and pregnant daughters, before her mother and her talkative friends had gotten the news. This prior knowledge had convinced Blanche's mother that her child had second sight.

Everything I was then, I am today. Blanche examined the idea and discovered all of her Night Girl courage and daring still in the safe in the back of her brain and growing more valuable every day. Without even realizing it, she drew on it when she needed to, like at the courthouse. Her break from there might turn out to have been a crazy thing to do, or it might not. In either case, it was the act of a take-charge kind of woman. A Night Girl kind of woman. Too bad she didn't also have the second sight her mother claimed for her. She could use it to make some sense of what Nate had said. She couldn't dismiss it. A black man in America couldn't live to get that old by being a fool. Tomorrow. She'd tackle him then. She yawned, said goodnight to the night, and went up to bed.

She lay naked on top of the sheets, hoping to attract a bit of the breeze she could hear stirring the pine trees. Despite the coolness of the evening, her high, narrow room was still full of afternoon warmth. She wondered if Taifa and Malik were asleep. She could see their round, plump faces, replicas of their daddy's sloe-eyed Geechee good looks. Did they suspect something was wrong? Kids were so good at feeling out situations.

She fell into a fitful sleep in which she was chasing a blood-red bus down a long, narrow highway and was in turn being chased by Mumsfield. Trees with prison matron branches reached out for her, but she knew she'd be safe as long as she kept moving.

"What do you think, Blanche? I trust you, Blanche!" Mumsfield shouted from behind. But she couldn't spare the breath to respond.

Up ahead, Malik and Taifa beckoned frantically from the back of the bus. She was carrying Mumsfield's automobile tools under her left arm.

Instead of her own hair, big, fat gray sausage curls flopped about on her head.

GWENDOLYN M.
PARKER

GWENDOLYN M. PARKER was born in and spent her early childhood in Durham, North Carolina, in a close-knit African-American community. She says that relatives were everywhere, "cousins filled the block, my grandmother lived in the house behind ours, and everyone knew everybody else's business, for better or for worse." When she was nine, she moved with her family to Mt. Vernon, New York, "ending up on a block with one aunt around the corner, and the other one almost across the street."

She received her B.A. from Radcliffe College, and her J.D. and L.L.M. from New York University School of Law. She worked on Wall Street for nearly ten years, first at Cadwalader, Wickersham and Taft, and then as a director of marketing at American Express Company. She left to devote herself to writing. She currently resides in Connecticut, where she is working on her next novel. *These Same Long Bones* (Houghton Mifflin, 1994) is her first novel.

As SOON AS I LEARNED to read, I remember thinking, I want to do this. I thought that it was an incredible thing to be able to create an experience, to create a world. There's a story that my grandmother always used to tell about me—that I once went through the neighborhood, house to house, with a little pad and pencil asking our neighbors questions, and then pretending to scribble their answers down on my pad. Of course I didn't know how to write yet, but that didn't bother me in the least. It was exciting just to imitate the process.

When I did eventually learn how to write, I would often write poetry about my feelings or observations. Writing for a living was a dream that I had, but that never seemed a realistic option as I was growing up. I didn't know any writers, and no one ever said to me, "You should be a writer." They said, "Oh, you love words and writing and reading, you should be a lawyer." My family was very achievement oriented. The underlying message was always: work hard at something that will bring you assured success. Given the realities of a racist society, assured success meant doing something where the rules are much more objective than they are with writing.

I rebeled only briefly against that message. After I got out of college in Boston, I moved to New York and tried to establish a career as a stage actress. For a black woman actress at that time, nearly all of the roles were either for a maid or a prostitute. I did not fit the role of a prostitute because I was six feet tall and skinny, so no one was going to believe that I was particularly voluptuous. That left the maid roles. The idea alone of playing a maid was just too demeaning. My attempt at acting was, all in all, pretty half-hearted. That spring I applied to law school for the following fall.

It was the safe and secure thing to do, and once I was on that path, I was on it with a vengeance.

I once read an interview with Maya Angelou in which she talks about writing her first novel. She ended up doing it, she says, because James Baldwin had told someone that the way to get Maya to do something was by telling her she couldn't. She said that she had this thing in her that would come out whenever someone told her she couldn't do something. I used to have that same thing in me. Maybe it was because I was angry that I wasn't really doing what I loved. Or maybe I was out to prove something.

I remember when I first moved here from the South, I felt that I needed to prove myself to the white teachers I had because they assumed that I was intellectually inferior and less educated. It seemed that I was always coming up against people who thought, "Oh, you can't do this." I got a C once on a poem I wrote in the sixth grade because the teacher said it was so good I must have copied it from some other source. He couldn't find that "other" source, but said he was giving me a C anyway because he knew I must have cheated. Experiences like that made me more and more frustrated and angry, and one day I decided that I was going to play by "their" rules, with the intention to win. I became bound and determined to do whatever was going to most confound people's expectations of what a black woman should be doing.

After law school, I chose to work at a very prestigious, WASPy, Wall Street law firm, because that was not where a black woman was expected to be. Once I was there I chose tax law, which was considered the most arcane and difficult of laws. I used to get a real kick out of going to all the meetings where there was a room full of much older white males, who I knew were thinking, What are you doing here? When they found out that I was a tax attorney, their looks would change to surprise, and then respect, in spite of themselves. I have to admit that it was very important to feel as though I had successfully beaten them at their own game. At the same time, it was also wearing.

I came from a family of businesspeople. My father, my great-aunt, and my great-uncle, each had their own drugstore. My great-grandfather started the first black-owned insurance company, one of my grandfathers started his own grocery store, the other was a real estate developer and banker. But they were not at all like the business people who I encountered in the larger white society. I realize, in retrospect, that part of what made me curious about business was to see the difference between how business was run in my family growing up and the big white world of business. I think I naively expected it to have some of the same dynamics, ethics, and relevance to its community—interconnection with other things. In my community growing up, the business people, the church people, the teachers, were all part of the same team.

I was appalled when I saw how atomized the business part of society was from the rest of the social fabric, how completely unfettered by other considerations of morality and ethics. Everything was "the bottom line." And not even the bottom line in the sense of, "Well, we need this for some purpose that you can understand," it was just *more*. Everything had to be more, not even in relationship to anything. Not "We need more because then the whole community will rise up and we'll be able to build a hospital." Just abstract more. And I thought, Couldn't I have known that? I probably did know that on an intellectual level, but it was important to see it firsthand and to understand it on an emotional level.

I think I had this plan, somewhat vaguely formed, to do something that would ultimately allow me the financial security to do what I really wanted to do, namely writing. But as I was busy living this plan I realized that I could not separate and send off only part of myself to do work that I didn't enjoy. It had become all of me, and I suddenly became very frightened that I was going to look up and be on my deathbed, and I would not have done what I wanted to do. I thought, Which is more scary—leaving what I am doing and just saying, I don't know whether this will work, but I'm willing to risk it, or lying on my deathbed, thinking that I never did the one thing I really loved and wanted to do. When it reached the point where the second was more scary than the first, I quit my job as a director of marketing at American Express, where I had been working for eight years.

I had started out in the law department at American Express, but I left because it was more monotony than I could bear. I went into marketing, which allowed me to be more creative. But every day I would think, I don't want to do this, I don't want to do this. Now I actually feel lucky, because before I left, I was up for a vice presidency position as an executive assistant to the head of American Express. This position would have meant longer hours, and even more intimacy with a world that I no longer wanted to be part of. The selection had come down to myself and one other candidate. I didn't get the position, and I was shocked. It had never been in my experience to not achieve what I had set out to achieve. Not being selected for the position interrupted my way of thinking, which, up until that point, had been completely "success oriented." It gave me a new perspective, and I saw very clearly that failing was not the worst thing. I could fail and survive. What I could not survive, however, was failing to at least try to do what I loved, to give it my all. I left the corporate world so that I could write.

Once I started writing the happiness I felt was overwhelming, but I was also rigid and inflexible in terms of what my writing regime would be. For the first year all I did was write. I was up and writing by six-thirty in the morning, a break at nine-thirty, back at work by ten-thirty, and on and on throughout the day. Once again, I was out to prove something, but I was also out to slay some demons. One of those demons was from my college days, when I had been very undisciplined. I would cram for exams and papers, but during the semester I would stay up with my friends all night debating the existence of the universe, always sleeping through classes the next day. I knew I couldn't write a book that way. So that year when I first started writing, I was incredibly disciplined. I still am, but I think I was a little obsessive that first year. I'm a *little* looser now.

I feel very grateful as a writer to be able to do work that allows me to follow my own natural rhythms. I like to work really early in the morning. I like to take a nap in the afternoon. I always felt odd in terms of that body rhythm at other jobs. Some people I worked with would hang out at the coffee machine until maybe nine or nine-thirty, and then start their day. By that time, I've already been working for a few hours and I'm ready to take a break, go for a walk or something.

I've written two novels at this point. The first is *These Same Long Bones*. The second is still in the rewriting stages and without a title. I've also written two screenplays. One of them is based on the slave narrative of Harriet Jacobs, and I am very pleased with it. After I finished the first novel, I really wanted to be working on something else right away. If I wasn't writing, it felt wrong. I knew that I wasn't ready to launch into another novel because it is so all-consuming. Someone who had read the first novel described it as being very visual and suggested that I think about writing a screenplay. It has been a good break for me in between novels. It uses a very different part of my imagination.

A screenplay is really something you give to the director and to the actors as a guide for their craft. It is so much more of a collaborative process. I didn't have the same kind of investment in the screenwriting as I did in the novel writing because I knew that other people were going to bring something of their own to a screenplay. The novel presents the experience that the reader will have. Obviously the reader brings her own dimension to it, but there will not be this whole cast of other people involved.

I tried to write plays when I was in college, but there is something about that particular space that I don't get. Part of it may be that I'm very fooled by spatial relations. The playwrights I know, their two strongest talents are dialogue and a strong sense of the theater space, and how to manipulate that space. I think my strongest suits are characterization and visual imagery. The visual imagery in a theater is much more three-dimensional.

What comes to me first when I write is a person, in a place, with something that has just happened, and an incredibly strong kinesthetic feeling that I have about that person, place, and what has happened. My immediate reaction is that I want to know, How did they get here and where are they going? It's this whole big arc that I am interested in. I think of poetry as being more zen, if you will, much more the present moment, which is an arc too, but poetry takes the present moment and makes it into a crystallized representation of a whole span of experiences.

I have a terrible memory for details, although I do store things emotionally. I remember that I read something and then can never remember what it was. I can remember whether or not I liked it, but can never remember who wrote it. I was a voracious, not very discriminating reader when I was young. I read whatever was around. When I began to notice who it was that I was reading, I remember that I really loved Pearl Buck and John Steinbeck. I loved their compassion. I'm afraid to go back and look at their books now. Maybe I wouldn't like them as much, and I would hate to lose that intense memory.

When I was about eleven, my parents enrolled me in a special course at a local college for gifted kids. We read a lot of Greek and Roman classics. I really loved *Beowulf*, it felt like reading a dream. I think part of it was that there is a certain consciousness that I relate with, much more so than where the book is set, or who the people are that the book is about. It never particularly bothered me that the people I was reading about weren't exactly like the people I knew. I'm more attentive to what someone's spirit is like, what their consciousness is like.

I really loved Willa Cather for her sense of connection between place and character, which is very important to me in my writing. I think that the quality of the light, where it is coming from, what the air is like, what the temperature is like, what trees are in your peripheral vision, have a very major impact on a particular moment. I tend to like books that have that element of connection between character, emotionality, place, and a sense of community.

I also really loved Dostoyevsky because of his attentiveness to the minute shifts of feeling and thought. His books are practically all interior. So much of what's important in his work is about how the characters are feeling and what they are thinking. I don't like books that are only about what happened, in terms of the plot sort of galloping along. I want to know *why* did it happen, and *how* did it happen.

Both before and after I've written something, the feeling of interconnectedness with other black women writers is certainly an assurance. The fact that these other voices are there, and that they are strong and available, gives me confidence to sit down and express my voice. I don't think anything provides assurance while I'm writing. I think in order to write I have to leap off the precipice over and over again. So when I'm doing that, there is no one there, including my own self. I have to leave behind who I was yesterday. I have to leave my own preconceived notions of what should happen next and where these characters should go.

The most supportive aspect of the community of black women writers for me is a certain tolerance for the individual, a tolerance for different truths. People operate at very different levels of consciousness. I remember when I first read Toni Morrison, I was in awe of her mastery of the written word. It's breathtaking. Her emotional power and perception, the minute shifts and the complexity of her characters are all so accurate about how people really are. Morrison requires a great deal of attention and awareness, truth seeking and soul searching. Some people aren't interested in engaging a lot of their energy in that, or would have the energy but don't choose to spend it that way.

For example, the kinds of things that some writers attend to in their work are more accessible to a larger number of people because the work more accurately represents how they constitute the world. Whereas Toni Morrison might be thinking about how what we say has something to do with something that happened a hundred years ago, and how it might be emblematic of what she sees as our own personal histories. Someone could read that and say, "Why is she going on and on about that?" Because it's not interesting to them, they don't pay attention at that level. Just like someone could look at this room we are sitting in and see its makeup in terms of what brand names the furniture and decor represent, someone else might look at it in terms of the palette of colors, someone else would really be interested in what it is that we are saying to each other.

I don't make a judgment about one being better or worse than the other, but the person who attends to a certain level of detail is going to want to read a writer who represents a similar level of detail for them. I think that the *modus operandi* in this society is to be half asleep, and that it is rare and difficult for people to be really awake. Writers who see that as their charge or their mission, who really want to represent what an awake world looks like to them, are not going to find the kind of readership of people who aren't as interested in sort of shaking up and turning upside down how things are viewed. And that is true among white writers, among black writers, all writers. There are lots of reasons why some very popular writers sell as many books as they do. Some of these reasons may be that they attend to stories and certain details that replicate television, modern movies, and, in general, the level of awareness and the attention span that a lot of people in this country have.

There is also a certain spirituality I feel from black women writers. Spirituality to me is a belief in the animated world—a world that has a life force, that permeates all of it, and a unity. Some people would call that God, some people would call that Buddha. There are different religions that I have read about and that I have practiced, but in terms of my own belief I don't feel the need to give a name to it. It is a belief in a unified source. A force that is in the trees, in each of us, in the air. A force that is available for us to go to, to learn from, to be nurtured by, nourished by, and most important, to be responsible to.

So many of the divisions we have come from people denying that existing force. Because if you accept that level of unity, then a lot of the things that we do don't make any sense. There is a fiction in western society that things are separate. People think that they can arm themselves, get guns, and build more prisons, do all these things that they think will insulate themselves against all the "violent others" out there. If they realized their connection to those "violent others," if they recognized them as part of the human family and acknowledged the essential unity, then they would see things very differently. It's a gradual process that usually begins with fear. It's frightening to be awake, because you have to be aware that there is this unity, but you are also in this life separate from it. It's exhilarating too. As a society, we don't help people over the scary parts. In fact we go the other way, we give people destructive ways of managing their fear. We are afraid of our essential aloneness and our essential connectedness, and the responsibility that brings.

There is a tolerance of different truths among the community of black women writers that is also not exclusive to black women. If we let people imagine "Your group is separate, you're different from these other people," then that group is better than that group, and their insecurities are appeased. Prejudice is a way of people managing fear and difference. And I think that people always know that their prejudices are not true. I think that racists know that they are not superior. It's a destructive cycle because it doesn't give any real assurance of what your ultimate fears are, so it's like a compulsion that has to be repeated.

Being awake gives you life. Every time you choose not to be awake, you die a little bit. You don't really feel the sunshine. You don't really feel love. We can't selectively shut off, so that when we do shut off to something we don't want to know, we are shutting off to all of the joy and fullness in life. I've done it myself, and I know how gradual and insidious a process it is. The trade-offs are—you get to have money if you choose not to know, you get to have this and that. Unfortunately the bargains are always less fulfilling than they appear. People think that what they are going to get back is going to make it worthwhile, but it never is, so you have to get more. If the bargains were ever what they said they would be, then you would have what you wanted and that would be that.

Ultimately, I think everyone gets flack for being an individual. In reality, the more skills that you have in trying to deal with the world wanting you to be A, when your spirit says you are B, the better off you are. I feel I have derived a certain amount of strength as an African-American because I never assumed that I would be like everyone else. I learned the lesson early on how to be myself. I have seen a lot of people who went along throughout their lives following all the rules, and then when they got older, decided that they needed to break those same rules in order to feel good about themselves. What they discovered is that they were totally unprepared to deal with being on the outside, and felt angry and cheated in a way that I have rarely seen people behave who have had the experience of being "outside."

It's important for any person who may be in a different situation from the norm to think about the choices they make. Parents especially have an obligation to provide our children with an environment that will be supportive. Because that way, when the children have to go to places that are not supportive, they can always come back to a secure base that is supportive and offers a broad range of experiences to draw from.

I have the ability to experience a permeable state similar to that which children experience, where the boundaries are not that firm yet. I am able to go very quickly into a stream of consciousness that children seem to be in all of the time. And I think that all writers have to be able to tap into some sort of flow. People have life themes. We come into this world with a charter for what we need to be doing here, as well as for our own individual growth. Those themes are very apparent and most intense during childhood, and less contaminated by our conscious minds, which is perhaps why many writers harken back to that time in their lives.

I think you come to your life theme again and again throughout your life. I can remember, when I was about five or six, having a very strong sense of the world as I've been describing it—the unity, the awesomeness, the interconnectedness, it was a very visceral experience for me as a child. I was very clear that I had a place here. Almost like seeing a map of the stars in the sky. I felt very secure. And that feeling has been re-created at different points in my life. Certainly the feeling was re-created when I was writing my first book. It felt like the completion of a circle.

From

THESE SAME LONG BONES

As if he'd been shaken, Sirus McDougald abruptly opened his eyes. There was a merciful moment of forgetfulness. The sheet was tangled about his long legs. He lay for a second at the center of a haze, moist and open from sleep, his limbs relaxed and peaceful, the recollection of a smile still puddled at the corner of his full lips. It was near dawn, and Sirus had been dreaming. He had dreamed that nothing would ever awaken him again. He had dreamed that he could stop life at his bedroom door. He had dreamed that he could force time to retrace its steps. But even as he turned to avoid it, the sun stole into his room, creeping into his sleep.

Sirus rubbed a broad hand across his face and looked drowsily around him. The dust in a beam of light that streamed through the blinds sparkled like fireflies near his slippers. Next to his head, on the small folding table he used as his nightstand, the light caressed the items he had laid out the night before: a small tortoiseshell comb, his pocket watch, his mother-of-pearl studs edged in gold, the loose pieces of paper on which he'd absently scribbled as he spoke to the reporter from the local paper. The light seemed to halt on the words on the top sheet of paper—"Brown, brown, 5'3", reading." What could the reporter he'd spoken to yesterday possibly print that would be news?

At once, Sirus's lingering ease was gone. His eyes widened, his chest swelled with air, and his mouth opened, gaping. He seized the piece of paper from the table, crumpled it, and stuffed it into his mouth.

A moan escaped. His daughter, his precious girl, his only child, was dead. Of what importance was the color of her hair and eyes, her height or favorite hobby, when even the paper boy knew more than that: knew that she liked to sit in the narrow tunnel made by the honeysuckles between their house and the Senates', knew how she banged out of the house with her skates already on, how she stopped on the grass at the edge of the walk to tighten them, knew the way she posed to wave good-bye, one hand on her hip, the other straight in the air, an elongated little teapot.

No, there was no news to convey, talking to the reporter was just a formality, one among dozens that were expected of him. So he rented all ten of Jason's cars for the funeral and he called people personally with the news, and he readied his house as if for a party. These were the things that were done, and he did each of them, when it was time, in turn. He knew that his neighbors and friends were similarly busy: the women baking pies and hams and fretting over who might not know and still need to be told; the men collecting money, arranging for their own transportation and clean black suits; even the children, bent over basement tables, cutting construction paper to serve as backings for paper flowers and poems.

Sirus forced his legs stiffly to the edge of the bed. Get up, he said to himself, spitting the paper onto the floor.

Outside, cars slowly traveled past his house. Some carried strangers: a Northerner in search of a relative's home, vacationers from farther inland heading for the coast, a delivery truck with vats of sweet cola syrup. But most carried Sirus's friends and acquaintances, unable to resist taking an extra turn past his house in an attempt to catch a glimpse of him or to see the large black and purple wreath hung on the door.

How was he holding up? Why was his wife, Aileen, sleeping over at her mother's house? Had they, following the country way, covered the mirrors with black paper? Like Sirus, the people who had settled this part of town—the colored section, which butted up against the white part of town and then turned back on itself—were primarily the descendants and relatives of farmers. As they'd spread throughout the city, one brother and then one cousin following the next, they'd left the country but brought their country ways: an unflagging belief in cause and effect—after all, hadn't they always reaped what they sowed—leavened by a large measure of fatalism bred by bugs, fire, and a too hot sun, and bound together by clannishness based on proximity, shared cheekbones, and common values. For these farmers and their progeny, holding the line against the sorrow of history, there was absolute virtue in hard work, an education was a lifeline, and life was an inevitable mystery. These things were givens, like the choice of good land, from which everything else that was good would proceed. And to these descendants of farmers, death itself was both sower and reaper, an unreasoning though sometimes benevolent messenger from God.

Sirus himself was born on a farm that produced three hundred baskets of tobacco a season, in a town called Carr, in the upper coastal plain of North Carolina. It was a typical pocket of life in the South, crammed with contradictions and ellipses of time. There were the Cherokee and the Tuscarora, who had lived on the land for always; the slave and the free Africans, who'd settled beside them; and the Scottish farmers, who had worked beside the others. Sirus's parents, like those of his neighbors, were descended from these Africans, Cherokee, Tuscarora, and Scots, and these people, when they were not farmers, were blacksmiths, barbers, cabinetmakers, grocers, and traders. They built everything they would have one day from these skills. And Sirus absorbed in his greens and hog crackling and corn bread the peculiar mixture of building and dreaming that was the heritage of these people. Now, in the wake of death, he was as much a part of this town of some five thousand colored people as the red dirt that ringed the manicured lawns, or the North Carolina light that was at once bright and hazy, or the ash, willow, cedar, and pecan that were native to the land.

Sirus stood now, some thirty-five years past his birth, in the late summer of 1947, in this town of Durham, North Carolina, which bustled with progress, in a house on Fayetville Street that was one of dozens he'd built, wishing he were the one who was dead. From his bathroom, the sun streaming in the window, Sirus could still hear the cars as they slowed to pass his house. He stood his shaving brush on its base, bristles up, to dry, and carefully shook the last drops of water from his razor. He looked at his face, now clean-shaven, in the mirror.

There was still the familiar broad chin, the wide cheekbones, the long thick nose, the thick black hair that formed a sharp contrast to his unbearably light, almost pearl-toned skin. The cold water had restored some color to his face; his gray eyes were smooth and clear. He marveled at his own composure. How could his features reveal so little while he felt as if every aspect of him, every thought and desire, every feeling and habit, was hurtling inside him at such speed and with such force that he could be an atom exploding, shattering into oblivion?

From the moment he had learned of Mattie's death, from each second that moved forward, he was dragged backward, caught in a great rush of time away from the present, away from the husband he'd been, the prosperous businessman the town had grown to rely on, the solid friend that so many came to for advice. And in his place loomed the specter of another Sirus, a youth, a boy he believed was long gone, a boy who was all quiet and softness. This boy, his eyes permanently wide, followed after him in his own house, relentlessly padded after him in his own shoes.

There had been nothing authoritative about Sirus as a child. He had been thin and too pale, his elbows always at the wrong angles, his energy too volatile, kinetic, as likely to lead him in one direction as another. But as the years went by his skin had gained a translucence and his energy had cohered, coalesced, so that it no longer erupted jerkily in his limbs but rode high in his chest, girded by his thickening muscles. As a man, he was loose-gaited, solid but warm. If he wanted to command attention, he had only to stand, releasing heat into the air like fire.

He dropped his gaze from the mirror to the basin and watched the spot where the water continued to run. A small green stain glinted at the bottom of the bowl. On any other day it was just green, a color, but today it summoned half a dozen memories: the color of new tobacco in the fields, the color of his mother's eyes when she stood in the light on their porch, the transparent color of an old penny, or the color, in spring, of all the land of his youth. The color, this green, came rushing up at him with its freshness and longing, setting off an embedded charge. Sirus doubled over, an intense wave of pain and nausea gripping his gut. He grabbed the sink, shaking.

Tears welled up and just as quickly receded. With careful steps he returned to the bedroom, took a clean shirt from his wardrobe, and slid his arms into the cool, crisp cotton. Then, slowly, he walked to the window. The starch in his collar was exactly as he'd requested, but now it felt like a gag. He watched the cars continue in an endless procession out on the street, until a black limousine appeared. It was Etta Baldridge's car, turning onto Fayetville from Dupree, already bearing down the road with that ominous cadence reminiscent of halting steps stumbling toward death. If its head-lights had been on, it would have looked as if it were already part of the funeral procession.

As the car crept down the street, Sirus could easily imagine Etta's voice and her short, sharp fingers tapping on the back of the front seat right below her driver's neck. "Albert, Albert, slower," she'd be saying. From where Sirus stood at the window he could imagine Etta's head, peeping forward from the relative darkness of the back of the car, her mouth moving animatedly, her face nearly pressed against the window. "Albert." Etta had been the first person to call on him when he had moved into this house. "I'm Etta Baldridge. Welcome to Fayetville," she'd said, pressing her face against the inside screen at the front door, an unofficial welcoming committee. Etta was always one to be pressing.

He thought he heard his housekeeper's key in the lock downstairs. Thank God, he thought. Mrs. Johnson could talk with Etta if she insisted on stopping. He reached for his pants from his wardrobe and his suspenders from the back of the cane-bottomed chair by the window. He knew that if he went out to the porch, Etta would ask Albert to stop altogether, would wave her arms and hands frenetically until he came out to the car. Once he was there, she would clasp him with those same grasping hands, her eyes sweeping greedily over him, hunting for a stain on his shirt, a cut from shaving, some food left on his lips, some sign of his grief— anything she could carry away with her to the bank or the insurance office or the beauty parlor where she would find an ear in which to deposit her find. If Etta saw him at this moment she might also be able to spy the child who was hiding in his face. He reached for his suit jacket, feeling a wave of relief as the car passed.

CHARLOTTE

WATSON SHERMAN

C

HARLOTTE WATSON SHERMAN

was born and raised in Seattle, Washington. She received her B.A. in social sciences from Seattle University. She has worked as a jail screener, sexual and domestic abuse counselor, creative writing workshop facilitator, and child welfare caseworker.

In 1989 Sherman received an Individual Artist award for fiction from the Seattle Arts Commission and the Fiction Publication Award from the King County Arts Commission. She received a 1991 Seattle Artists grant, and a 1993 literary fellowship from the Washington State Arts Commission.

Killing Color, a collection of stories delicately exploring otherworldly dimensions of African-American experiences, published in 1992 by Calyx Books, won the Great Lakes Colleges Association Fiction Award and a Governor's Writers Award in 1993.

Her first novel, *One Dark Body,* was published by HarperCollins in 1993. She is currently editing an anthology of short fiction and poetry by African-American women.

DIDN'T COME TO WRITING, writing came to me. I remember as a kid trying to re-create stories that I had read. I wanted to write, but I don't remember having a concept of what a writer was, much less a black writer. I never had any models. I thought that if there were such a thing as being a writer you had to be from Harlem. How many black writers do you know from Seattle? James Baldwin was the first black author I read, but that wasn't until high school. I didn't start reading black women writers until I got into college, where I had a professor who introduced me to writers like Zora Neale Hurston, Alice Walker, and Maya Angelou. I began to think about being a writer only once I started to read these black women writers. I can't remember wanting to do it in a public way, I think it was something that I wanted to do more for myself.

I wrote this poem in college called, "In Memory of African Youth" which was published by both *Black Scholar* and *Obsidian*. The poem came from the rape of one of my brother's friends by two white men. It was a really hard time and a very painful experience, and I was grateful to be able to catch an essence of it in the poem. I'm still proud of that poem. That's when I started feeling like the writing was real. I kept writing poetry up until about five or six years ago, when the poems started getting longer. That's when I began writing fiction instead. I went from these longish poems to would-be short stories.

After I really experimented with the medium for a while, I put together *Killing Color*, a collection of short stories. Then I wanted to write a novel. *One Dark Body* is the product of that desire. The type of writing that I attempted to do in that novel is magical realism; it's what you find in Toni Morrison's work, or August Wilson's work, or Latin American and Native American writers, as well as African writers, where there's a blending of the real with the unreal, the seen with the unseen. That blend is challenging and intriguing to me.

The story itself came to me in a few different ways. The title came from a quote from W.E.B. Dubois's *The Souls of Black Folk:* "One ever feels his twoness—an American, a negro; two souls, two thoughts, two unreconciled strivings; two warring ideals in one dark body, whose dogged strength alone keeps it from being torn asunder."

The idea of being double-sighted, that kind of schizophrenic reality that we as African-Americans have in this country. The phrase "two warring ideals in one dark body" made me sure that I wanted to write something called *One Dark Body*. There is also the story of one of my relatives whose mother left her with another woman to raise. When the mother came back for her later, the woman who raised her would not give her back to her mother. The mother ended up dying at an early age, and I heard the child, as an adult, recall the incredible loss she felt even though she never really knew her mother. That was an interesting story to me. At that time, I was also working as a case worker for the state with children who had been abandoned by their parents. So I was really able to see and explore some of the issues and emotions around abandonment. Those are all the ways in which the story came to me and the ideas I drew upon to keep it alive.

As I was growing up in Seattle, Washington, my brothers and myself were usually among the few people of color at the schools we attended. Out of a school of three hundred kids, there may have been ten or fifteen black students. In our classes, the only references made to black people had to do with slavery. No other world contributions by black people were mentioned except that we were slaves. I remember feeling terribly ashamed.

Although my parents were from the South, they did not talk a lot about their past or the racism that they had experienced there. Moving to Seattle they hoped would allow them to create a life for themselves and their children less reminiscent of southern racism. But, of course, there were many situations my brothers and I encountered that were racist. For example, one of our classmates who wouldn't allow us to come inside her house but would let white children in. These types of occurrences were very real, but as kids, we just felt a strange sort of confusion.

Growing up as one of a few, I grew up feeling a strong sense of invisibility. That sense developed into a real *desire* not to draw any kind of attention to myself whatsoever. Though I had white friends in elementary school, once I entered junior high school, white friends became socially unacceptable to other black students at the school.

When I was in ninth grade, I stole *The Autobiography of Malcolm X* from the school library. Until that point, I had always had the impression that white people were right about everything and that black people were somehow wrong. After reading *Malcolm X*, I understood that African-Americans were not the ones who needed to feel ashamed. That *I* didn't need to feel ashamed. That was a liberating moment.

I became a voracious reader, which made me very odd in my family. My parents were working-class people who didn't read much besides the Bible, the Daily Racing Form, the newspaper, and some magazines. My mother thought I read too much, and that I wasn't healthy because of it. Although they are happy about my writing now, both my parents thought my interest in writing and reading as a kid was strange, and that my strangeness would only heighten the difficult situation I was already in as a black female. But reading took me all over the world, and I insisted on doing it.

Reading took me to different places, languages, experiences, sights, sounds, tastes—things that were not in my immediate world but that I could get to through books. I have always been curious about exploring the world throughout my life, especially since I've never really left Seattle. Deciding to write was not intentional, and I made no pretense to that effect. I didn't expect that I was going to take anyone anywhere, as I had been taken by other people's writing. I read something, put it down, and tried to do the same. It was something that made me feel good inside.

I like fiction because I can create characters and situations that I can hide behind. Hiding creates a feeling of safety for me. It is hard for me to reveal myself in my writing. I am much more interested in listening to other people's stories. Right now I am supposed to be writing an essay about living and writing in the Northwest for an anthology—and it's difficult. I'm having real trouble with it. When I'm writing, I feel like I am free—it's exhilarating and wonderful. But when my writing is published and becomes public, then it's an entirely different feeling. I still haven't gotten to the point where I feel comfortable standing behind my work and saying, "This is what it is." I still have to fight this feeling that I have to apologize.

I don't know where that feeling comes from. Having had this conversation before with other black women writers, I think that for many of us, especially those of us who grew up in families where we weren't necessarily encouraged to be anything artistic or intellectual, and were viewed as strange because we *were* interested in that sort of thing, we have now reached a point as adults where we create our art. We put it out there and are terrified about how the world will react to it. Because we really don't have the slightest idea what the response to the work will be. Since we were made to feel so strange about wanting to do something artistic, that makes us keep the writing close to our hearts. I think what makes me able finally to put it out there is being attached to the idea of seeing it in its finished form, in a concrete way, something I can hold. Like a book.

The strength to keep on publishing comes from knowing that Toni Morrison is doing it too, that Ntozake Shange is doing it. That we are all doing it. The kind of emotional territory that Toni Morrison covers in her work is profound, and her skill is extraordinary. Ntozake Shange embodies a sense of positivity and strength regarding African-Americanness and femaleness, and the way she intertwines those two elements in her work has been a major influence on me.

The way that I try to intertwine that duality in my own writing is to reverse the negativity around darkness—the way black is always equated with evil, and dirtiness, and how everything horrible in the world is always black or dark. I'm certainly not the first person who wanted to work with reversing that kind of imagery, but it is tremendously important to me. Another thing that I try to do is to explore ritual. I'm really interested in how women don't have rites-of-passage experiences in this country anymore. So I try to research those rites of passage that are lost, especially elements from traditional societies where we can go back and see and learn and talk about these types of things in a group setting, and intrinsically feel the value of what we are—the value of femaleness, the value of the feminine. I feel this is important for us especially now, all you have to do is look at the rap music industry. There are a lot of young female rappers who refer to themselves as bitches and hoes, and that makes me feel that we are so cut off, particularly women, but society in general too, from valuing the feminine. So I hope that I succeed in addressing that in my writing.

I define and deal with blackness and femaleness on a personal level. My sense of self comes from knowing that I am connected with a long history of people and especially women who have struggled. Women who, no matter what, made a way for themselves and for their families, and were able to keep going. Women who gave enough of themselves so that we now have a foundation to draw from and to build on. A lot of times when I feel overwhelmed or like I can't do something, I think about the black women who did things when they didn't have any of the opportunities that I have now. So I don't really have any excuses. I also have some close friends who are black women writers. We are mirrors for one another and affirm one another's lives. The black women writers I don't know, I don't have to know personally in order to get a sense of pride and affirmation from their work, and encouragement to keep doing what I am trying to do, in my writing and in my life.

There are moments, *those* moments, that make me sure I'm doing the right thing in my work. Once I did a reading in Oakland, and afterward a woman came up and gave me a big hug. She thanked me for writing *One Dark Body*, and she talked about how it had helped her in her life. Her mother had died when she was young, and she had experienced feelings of abandonment. She had told her therapist about the book so she could share it with other people because she felt it was a healing story. It was a powerful story for me to hear, because when I'm writing, I'm way over on the other side and I don't know if people are going to be at all moved by the words I write. Or if I've done any good. So when something like that happens, I know for certain the reason I am doing what I am doing. I also met some people in D.C. not too long ago who actually collect the work of African-American women writers. To know that they were doing that and to be a part of the group whose work they were collecting was a wonderful moment. That also helped me to begin to take myself more seriously as a writer, and to realize that what I was doing was important.

At a reading for *One Dark Body* in Philadelphia, a man came up to me and said, "I got it! I got it! The *sin* is not to heal the wound!" And I thought, Yes, that's it! What he meant was that no matter what has happened to wound black people, individually or collectively, we have to go back and find a way to heal those wounds for the sake of our future generations. As a writer, I am connected to a tradition that is very crucial to black culture. The psychological and emotional wounds that we have as part of our history can be healed, perhaps through the writing.

I don't have an audience in mind when I write. If I envision people standing up behind me, watching me as I work, that will distract me, and maybe even stop me from writing. But on the other hand, I do think about young black children, coming up without any access to our history, to our words. I think about myself in grade school, wanting to read and being curious, and not being exposed to materials written by black people. So I guess if I think about anybody when I am writing, it would be an image of a young black woman, thirsty for knowledge and written words with which she can identify. That image is not as intimidating as one of a whole audience, and it also is stimulating because I know how I would have felt if I had had access to black words in writing when I was a young girl.

There are lots of times when I feel like I can't do it anymore, the writing that is. Like now. I have to write this next book. I have some ideas, but in the next month or so, I'm actually going to have to sit down and start working with them. I am always working in my mind with this idea of resistance to losing your soul, and I want to incorporate ritual with that idea as well—the passing between ages, that time of transition. I know that I hope to deal with some issues around aging and death. Who knows? I think that a writer can write one book or two books, or however many, but I still have to come up against the blank page, every time. That's a terrifying feeling. So far I've overcome it. I have to have faith that I'll do it again.

From
ONE DARK BODY
Nola

As Nola lay on the quilt-covered bed, she knew her days of waiting to put El to rest were coming to an end. Soon his bones could be still.

Light slid over her body in wide-slatted bars. She heard the soft-throated call of doves blessing the woods, the long honking laughter of black-necked geese, the muted peeps of other gentle praising birds.

She smoothed the shell of her body, which softened like dark cloth under the iron of her hands.

She felt all the days of her life in Pearl sitting like a low-slung sun inside her belly, turning the water inside her mouth pickley hot.

The room filled with memories smelling of red cedar and sage, a dry, burning, man's smell. El.

She closed her eyes, took a long breath and eased his heavy scent inside her body as if she were again learning who he was. The pure, sure lines of his nose, the soft black mat of hair covering his cheeks and chin, the full lips that opened like a strongbox of dark hope.

She remembered the day in the woods when she had leaned against a soft-barked tree and pulled El close to her slowly swelling body. Remembered the smell of hot foliage, remembered her hands holding the domes of his shoulders underneath his shirt, the slow drag of fingertips across the rising island of flesh that was his birthmark.

She had rested her body on El. Laid the weight of her life at their feet, closed her eyes and rested.

Nola remembered the stern face of Ouida Barnett rising out of the darkness of her mind, a curious gleam in her eyes.

Nola had turned from her mother's frowning face shining before her eyes. Ouida Barnett's eyes bright with the light of disappointment, that bitter, wounding colored woman's disease.

Nola had packed the image of her mother away in a tight white box, back in a musty corner of her mind, as she slowly unbuttoned El's shirt.

The sight of his smooth black skin made her mouth water. She had been thirsting for love so long in her mother's house.

Nola drew her tongue over El's body until his skin began to liquefy.

She unbuttoned his blue jeans and slid them, over high round buttocks, down to his ankles.

She held his penis, swaying before her, lightly in her hands. She dropped and knelt on pine needles and leaves broken on the ground and took him into her mouth.

Her body swayed to the beat of El's frenzied rocking and moans until her tingling lips drew a cord of liquid pulsing light from inside him.

He had knelt before her then.

Dropped to his knees on the leaf-implanted ground and stroked her naked legs.

His lips brushed the insides of her knees and calves, before moving higher to the delicate flesh of her thighs, where he nibbled her skin until she hummed with pleasure.

Nola had pulled El's head to that part of her belly she could not see, but could feel, burning now, yearning for fusion, wanting the plunge of his sweet searching tongue.

The gentleness of his hands had unnerved her, as he caressed the dark rising beneath her dress like a waxing moon; each stroke, each circling of fingertips on her skin made her feel as if he were sculpting her and the baby out of the clay of their awaiting life together.

This was not the love of her mother, Ouida Barnett. Not a long seeking of self in other selves, not a great yawning gap of waiting empty.

This was not the curious love of her father, not the dull appreciation in his hypnotic, narcotic eyes.

The love she felt for El was a circle, a ring, a world; something that sprang from itself, full, spinning, free. A love as bright with darkness as a black hole dense with stars.

This was a feeling she thought she could grasp in her strong young arms and hold onto, something elusively solid, something real.

She remembered El talking about wanting to leave his body, El always telling her he really knew how. She had never believed him.

"The old folks know how. Them folks come over on them slave ships knew how. Some of em did it. Just laid down and was still. Let their souls walk away from their bodies till all that was left was the bones."

"You supposed to be here. You better keep both your feet on this ground. Don't quit on me."

"Something calling me, Nola. I can feel it calling."

"This your home, El. Our child right here in this world. In this belly. This one. Feel this."

El had ignored the gift of the belly she offered and kept on staring like he was looking on some other shining motionless world.

"You ever feel something pulling you, something liquid, gentle, sweet?"

"Not like you talking about. This our life. These my hands holding you."

"Something strong . . ."

"My love strong."

"Quiet. Whispery watery quiet. Peace."

"We'll make us a quiet place, find us a peaceful place in this world."

"I'm tired, Nola."

"You tired? You too young to be tired. You ain't even carrying the baby."

"But I'll be carrying that baby once it comes. I'm gonna haveta carry the load. Gonna get packed like a mule."

"We both gonna work."

"But I'm gonna haveta go down in them mines. Just like my daddy and all the other men around here. That's the only kinda work a colored man can do. Go down in a hole and dig. Get turned into some kinda sad sorry machine. Ain't you ever noticed how none of em talk about what it's like? Don't say nuthin about what it does to you going down into a hole every day. But I can see it, Nola. Even if they don't say. Living gonna suck on my life till ain't nuthin left but light behind soft black bones."

"What about the good in life, El? Me and the baby. Love? You know how your people think. How they say taking your own life's the same thing as murder. It ain't right. Your spirit won't ever find peace. They don't believe in nuthin like that."

"I can't carry you and the baby and what-all my people think the rest of my life. Ain't never gonna be free."

Nola felt the band breaking, saw the dull glow of a crumbling ring, smelled the circle make a slow rusty turn.

"We your people now, El. The baby and me. We could always work a while, then leave. Start over somplace else."

"Can't do it, Nola. I don't think I can go down in that hole and stay alive. Not here or noplace. That hole would be waiting on me anyplace else I'd go. Can't do it. Not for you. Not for nobody."

"Your people don't hold no stock in you trying to leave here and not coming back, El. Nuthin good gonna ever come from doing something like that. You won't never get no rest you do something like that, El. Not never. That's one of the worst things your people say you can do."

"Nobody gonna turn me into no shadow."

"We all tired, El. We all gonna be tired long as we keep living. Don't you see? We all gotta put our feet on this ground and grab hold of this life tight as we can. We ain't got no choice but to hold on. Make the best outta what we got. Try to do a good thing while we here. It ain't too much to ask. Ask your people what happen when you just let go."

Nola hadn't believed El was serious. She had hoped he was talking to hear himself talk. But El did not ask his people anything, he had simply opened his arms and let go. They found his body in a shallow grave he had dug for himself out in the woods, wrapped inside a dirt-covered white sheet, once-strong arms, floppy on his chest, not far from the long-legged tree where he and Nola had often made love.

■

Nola had left her body then. Sucked into the middle of fast, furious winds, she floated inside the eye of herself, a great white eye inside herself, where she found a still place, a sharp white place, where nothing moved.

Nola lived her life from the center of that stillness, that blinding silent fury, that white unblinking eye.

She remembered walking to the grave El had dug for himself, the spot of tranquility he had longed for, the place where he had willed his soul to walk away from his body and leave him without substance, light or shadow in a hole in the ground, that tight-lipped womb whose dark hold was more lasting than hers.

She had dropped to the ground and pressed her full belly into the soft dark earth.

"Can You hear me, El? Can you hear? I am bringing you this, bringing you all of me, all that is me, the swelling bowl of my life, like gold, I am bringing you the sun in my heart, a white slip of moon in my grin, bringing you the dark petals of my life, my legs, my crooked yellow toes, I am bringing you my river of laughter, the sharp sea of my sweat when we love, bringing you my rambling tongue, my fat kisses, my one eye that never blinks, I am bringing you my hips that rock, shake, sing, bringing my fists and sharp elbows, my short fingernails, crazy eyebrows, the lashes that will bald when I'm old, the curious world inside my head, I am bringing you, bringing you me, all of me on this platter of earth, your earth, the place you call home, now, honey, sugar, your true love, the place where you find comfort in another's dark arms, I am bringing you this, bringing you all of this . . ."

BARBARA

SUMMERS

BARBARA SUMMERS was born in Spring-field, Massachusetts, grew up in Hartford, Connecticut, and graduated from the University of Pennsylvania in 1965. Summers completed course work toward a doctorate in French literature at the Graduate School of Yale University. In 1967, with the help of a John Hay Whitney Fellowship, Summers went to live and study in Paris. In 1972, she settled in New York City with her son. Summers taught French and journalism at Medgar Evers College in Brooklyn before starting a seventeen-year career as a fashion model with the Ford Agency in 1973.

In 1989, Summers was the editor for the critically acclaimed *I Dream a World: Portraits of Black Women Who Changed America* by Brian Lanker. *Nouvelle Soul,* a collection of her short stories, was published in 1992; *The Price You Pay,* a novel, in 1993; and *Skin Deep: The Story of Black Models,* in 1994, all by Amistad Press. Ms. Summers lives in Teaneck, New Jersey.

T WASN'T DIFFICULT TO edit the text for *I Dream a World* because I was curious about the women involved. I didn't come to it with a lot of preconceived ideas. The biggest help was that Brian Lanker took the photographs of the women and did the interviews as well. So I had these wonderful black-and-white portraits of individuals while I was dealing with the transcripts. What was hard was trying to distill a thousand words from hours and hours of conversation, which was strictly for the material package of the book. Otherwise, as I hope is evident from just the excerpts, each one of those women deserves at least one book to herself.

Those black women are in the book because they did something fascinating. They don't have to be larger than life, although Toni Morrison has that wonderful expression, "What can be larger than life?" There is something about each woman that makes her deserve a whole book, not just one page.

What I learned from the women in *I Dream a World* is that possibilities are endless. They all kept saying in one way or another that they could do anything they wanted to do. I always, sort of, basically, believed that too, but it took me a while to do something with that belief. I was going through a real rough period when I did that book, so to see these black women of all ages really activating that philosophy was very inspiring.

I had really wanted to do the project. I submitted a proposal, with a concept for the format of the text, like an audition. When I was hired to do it and began working closely with Brian Lanker, it was difficult because, since he knew the women, having interviewed them and photographed them, he thought he had a slight edge on me. But since I am a black woman, I didn't think his edge was more than what I knew. We did clash, though. He had a tendency to emphasize the poor, downtrodden, powerless, uneducated, and all there is to that side of our experience as black women. I'm not going to say it doesn't exist, but my tendency was to accept that it is there, and to then put it in the context where triumph is the ultimate end. Or not even necessarily triumph, but something splendid.

There were three editors who worked on the book—Lanker, the author and photographer; Maureen Graney, the in-house editor; and me. Both Lanker and Graney had limited experience with black culture. I was the only African-American on the project. That had been a tremendous incentive for me to work on the project too. I mean shoot, it's not that everybody considered it to be a blockbuster to begin with. I kept telling these people it was going to be a best-seller. They planned to come out with a 25,000 run. I thought, okay, that's respectable. But I knew how hungry black people were and are for documentation of our experience. This project was not just tokenly black, it was an artist's vision of us. And even though Lanker had just discovered black people himself, he still brought an originality and an authenticity to it that say, *Songs of My People*, does not have because it is not an artist's vision.

The editors with *Songs of My People* contracted fifty black photographers to shoot a day in the life of black America. The book is very jumbled, there is no coherent vision, and consequently, the artistic value of the photographs and even the page layouts is blown. But still, once again, we're so hungry, we're so eager. I'm sure the book is doing well, it's touring all over, just like *I Dream a World* toured. But there is no comparison between the two books' artistic quality.

I hope that *I Dream a World* inspires writers and editors to do similar projects for years to come. Let's not fool ourselves about what we are actually looking at though. Black people felt embarrassed that it took a white man to do this, to document our experience so accurately, and I say, "Hey, be embarrassed, and then go out and do a great job with a similar project." We all get tired of seeing black life portrayed through white eyes, most definitely, but we've got to do a better job portraying our own experience, or else white folks are going to keep on doing it.

I think maybe one of the things that black women writers are doing is reestablishing that our sensuality is valuable. It seems that if anyone believes in sensuality these days, in all of its indescribable and total omnipresence, it is only young people, and that's out of sheer naivete. Old people think in terms of materialism and money and security, they've been through life, they've had broken hearts, and they've had to live with them. Maybe sensuality exists in life in the same way that foreplay exists in sex, or maybe it's like the cocktails before the dinner, or the playing around before getting serious. Whatever it is, black women are definitely exploring all of the possibilities in our writing.

I believe sensuality is all around us—it's really hard to separate it from a total life consciousness. I am truly sorry that I feel it has been so devalued, but I am especially grateful to black women writers who have integrated it into their work. I think that sensuality is what keeps us, as black women, sane in an insane world. I'm not saying that our sensual awareness can solve everything, but to be in touch with it is important. Particularly as we live in a culture that *says* it is in touch with sensuality but isn't. The whole concept of models, for example, is a flagrant violation of what is really sensual.

I've just come off of seeing the Tina Turner movie *What's Love Got to Do with It?* I have such mixed feelings about it that I'm not sure I can even be articulate, but one of the things is that I get so tired of seeing downtrodden black women. We can be and we are, but we are also the most gorgeous people on the planet. You see these downtrodden black women in all the documentaries of black life, all the civil rights leaders are men, unless they bring in Fannie Lou Hamer with a busted eye in jail, or Rosa Parks, who is totally angelic and wonderful but not quite representative of the hard work that black women did to get where we are. The disempowered, victimized images are everywhere.

The book that I am working on now, *Skin Deep*, is about beautiful black women models. Straight out, straight up, beautiful black women who have made careers of being beautiful black women. Whose faces have been in the American media for the last fifty years. People think that only since the sixties have we had beautiful black women. No, uh-uh, we've been beautiful all along. It took us a long time to realize it, and took even longer for white America to realize it, but we are here.

I've been working on this book for seven years. There are no original illustrations in the book, it's all archival, taken from previously published photographs when these women were in their prime. My work room has a whole wall covered with these women, you set them up face by face, and they are all equally spectacular. We tend to think that our generation is just the best—but you look at these women and you're like, "These girls were baaaad! They were baaaad, they were flawless, they were fabulous!" And they were wonderful to talk with, too.

I started modeling in 1973 when I was twenty-eight years old, which is the age of retirement for most models. I lied about my age, and I didn't even want to do it in the first place. I had gone to the University of Pennsylvania for my undergraduate studies, and then to Yale for my graduate work. I had been a French major at Yale and had received a fellowship to study abroad in Paris. I never went to school during the three years I lived there, and I never went back to Yale to finish.

When I came back to New York with my new son, I got a teaching job at Medgar Evers College in Brooklyn. I was trying to be a positive person, but it was real difficult because I didn't like New York. I considered Paris *the* city, which didn't sit too well with Americans, especially African-Americans. My sister was working for *Mademoiselle,* and they were looking for working women. I had this little teeny, weeny Afro, scalp clean. And I was a vegetarian so I was real, real thin. The magazine liked me, and after doing a couple of shoots with me, told me I needed to get an agent. They sent me to Eileen Ford, who took one look at me and said, "Oh, this will never do." But when I started to walk out the door, she said, "Wait, let's see what we can put together." I signed on with her and stayed for seventeen years.

Modeling was very interesting work. I made a lot of money, went to wonderful places, worked with creative people—the clothes, the photographers, the art designers, the art directors, were all really something. It was a stimulating atmosphere. The only problem was, I couldn't say much. I was basically a walking prop. After a while, I wanted to use my brain.

I don't know exactly how I came to writing. My mother was a poet, and we always had a lot of books in the house. I liked to write as a kid and was always a closet writer, or a drawer writer—sticking it back in the drawer. Once I became an adult, I couldn't see how I was going to make a living as a writer. I liked teaching, that was cool, and my whole thing had been that I was going to be a Ph.D. in French by the time I was twenty-five. I was on my way, the only thing is, I started living in Paris. That sidetracked the whole thing. And I'm so glad it did. I wouldn't want to be all worried about tenure and getting reviewed now. I write about people like that.

I'm too irreverent for the establishment anyway. If you are an academic, you really have to tow the line, unless you come in as an eccentric. If you come in as an artist, it's a little different than if you come in as say, Skip Gates, somebody who is going to carry the mantle of the race on his shoulders. Also, if you're not a man in academe, you have to fight like one. There is enough just general hassling within the institution that you have to put up with, and then to be a black woman there—no, not for me.

I did start to write while I was in Paris because I didn't have to worry about making a living, which of course was one of the wonderful things about Paris at that time. But when I came back to the States, with this little baby, I *did* have to make a living. That's why I went into teaching. After a year of teaching, I went into modeling. And after seventeen years of modeling, I went into midlife crisis. During the midlife crisis, I said to myself, Okay, you modeled, that's an impossible profession, let's see about the writing.

I had been very despondent one summer, and I started writing short stories. And that is really what saved me. I don't even know why I chose short stories as the medium, people say it's so difficult, but it is the form that writing came to me in, so I trusted it. And still do. Nothing is easy to write, medium or message. I don't think of it in terms of what is easier. Things come to me. I get a line first, or an image, some sort of gift, and then I get to work. I can't sit until I get that gift, and then the struggle begins.

I have to be disciplined about my writing, otherwise there is no difference between *being* a writer and *saying* I want to be a writer. Everybody wants to be a writer. Although it is a lonely life sometimes. Often you are all holed up in a room without anybody to talk to for long periods of time. What keeps me writing is that I want to get better. The only way to get better is by keeping at it. There are a lot of stories I want to tell. And I do love writing. I love when a wonderful sentence comes as all one- or two-syllable words that anybody on the planet could understand if it was in his or her language. I'd love it if my audience was the whole planet.

My mother loves that I am a writer. She never made a living as a poet, but did publish one book. She still has the sensibility of a poet's approach to life, which is looking for beauty, looking for the unexpected—the human or the natural. It is not a very structured or materialistic vision, but very open and creative. It's a creative vision to the point of restructuring language for things you see or hear or smell. I don't think poets are necessarily more sensitive people, but they think they are, and that carries them a long way.

Poets act as though they are more sensitive, and most times really want to be. Again and again they take the risk because there is no alternative for them, and they are always crucified for it. I only have some of that in me. All of my earlier writing was poetry. Once in a while I fall back into it, but not with the dedication of a real poet, for whom poetry is primal. I would never call myself a poet. I will call myself a writer, and in that sense, I would hope that I could write anything.

Black women writers are in a world of our own. I am in awe of those around me. I don't write like any of them, I just adore them. Whenever Toni Morrison comes out with something, I just fall into it. I understand that some people in this country may have trouble reading Toni, because the language is so rich poetically, but if you can really get to it, what she is offering to literature is tremendous. And Alice Walker is that way too. She talks about how so many of our foremothers were not able to express themselves. I feel that our collective expression as black women writers today is for our foremothers as well as for ourselves.

I don't style myself after any other writers. They do what they do, and I do what I do. I don't want to write like Toni, I'd like to be as wise as she is, but I don't want to write like her. I don't want to intimidate anyone. I want everyone to be able to read what I write. I don't want to do a lot of posturing and philosophizing in my writing, which makes it more accessible to a larger audience. I really want to encourage people to get more into just reading. It's disturbing how few people read.

There are African-Americans who are so Afrocentric that if a book doesn't have red, black, green, or yellow on the cover, then they think that it's not going to be applicable to "the black experience." I don't like that. We can be African-Americans of all sensibilities and sensitivities. We have to be able to stretch to that. I also think that our literature needs to elicit more laughter. That's what I miss in the literature coming from the sisters and brothers. And that's why I consider Langston Hughes to be my spiritual father—Langston could make people laugh. That doesn't happen in black literature today. Ain't nobody laughin' out there. Although Terry McMillan has begun to do that. That's why she is so popular—she's making people laugh. We need more of that. Laughter is joyous, spiritual, and intuitive.

My sense of self changes every day. It's not carved in stone. It really isn't. I'm always trying new combinations. I don't want to limit myself as being any one thing. As a writer, I can be lots of different things. The actual physical descriptions of characters, the reactions to situations, locations, objects—I get a chance to have that God-like approach. I can be everything and am never limited. I decide.

The writing continues every day, and I am amazed. Sometimes I get concerned if I am away from it for too long, because I figure it's not very good if it's not compelling me to work on it every second of every day. But then I go back and read it, and it *is* good. Being a middle-age person but a young writer is hard, because one of the things that characterizes youth is impatience, and I am very impatient as a writer. But one of the things that characterizes middle age is patience, and so it's hard, because I don't want to hear myself say, "Slow down, everything comes in time." I want to get it all done now and right now.

From
NOUVELLE SOUL
A Bite to Eat

When Mama used to open for Miss Billie at The Green Door, she'd line us up on a bench in Gouverneur Park across the street, Chickie who was seven, Booboo who was only three and a half, and me. She'd say, "Bunny, you're in charge," sort of the same way she told me when I finally did turn ten that a double digit age meant I had to stand on my own two feet now.

She'd sit us right at the edge of the park with a brown bag still warm and heavy from fried chicken and biscuits and tell us, "Don't move, don't talk to strangers, and be good to each other." Then she'd give us a chord, an easy one like C major. Booboo held the C, I had the E, and Chickie had the high voice, so he got the G. And she'd say, "All right now, let me hear you hold it." We'd start off real good and try to stay that way while she walked to the club, patting her hat down and putting her gloves back on. She had such a pretty way of walking, skirt swinging like a satin metronome, high heels that crossed at the ankles. We couldn't help but watch her till she got to the door and waved back to us.

I always wanted to see just how long we could hold a chord, but soon as Mama was inside Chickie'd want to attack the bag. I'd say, "Chickie, you know we can't eat till three. It's only two o'clock now." And I'd show him on Daddy's round gold watch that he left me when he went overseas that the big hand had to go all the way around before the little hand would move to three. But I always gave him an apple or an orange, 'cause I wasn't too crazy about warm fruit myself. And that would keep him quiet while he worked on his coloring books. I'd read stories to Booboo or make them up myself, and she'd put her little head in my lap and suck her finger and smooth her nose and sort of take a nap. It was a good time.

Sometimes Miss Kitty, she was the one with the real blond hair, or Miss Candy, she was the one with the long wavy hair, would come and sit with us and smoke a cigarette between their dance routines. Then we could go on the swings and the slide for a few minutes. Miss Kitty taught me to shuffle-ball-change and was going to teach me more, but Mama said my shoes were getting scuffed up too fast, tap dancing in the street. They were good to us and smelled good to us and always left us with Chiclets or Life Savers, saying "Here's something sweet to remember me by." And when they went back to the club, sometimes we could hear just a few notes, Mama singing or the band swinging. They were having fun.

Nothing ever happened. Except one day.

One day we saw this big black Cadillac pull up to The Green Door, and this man and this lady with a dog got out. They were talking loud and fussing, and all of a sudden the lady ran toward the park where we were, all the while carrying this little dog. She sat down with a sad face and a loud noise on the bench right across from us. She looked at us and we looked at her. She could have been so pretty, but her face was twisted and her eyes looked dirty and wet. Still and all, we knew who she was. I mean, me and Chickie knew. Booboo was too young to know about Miss Billie Holiday.

We started talking across to each other at the same time. After all, she wasn't a stranger. She said, "Aren't you Hazel's children?" at the same time I said, "Is anything wrong, Miss Billie?"

We all sort of smiled at each other. I said, "Yes, ma'am." She said, "No, sweetheart, it's all right." Her little dog wiggled down and came over to us, sniffing around our brown bag. Chickie held on to it tight, but Booboo put her hand out to feel the dog's soft smooth hair. She was just a baby, but little things liked her and she was never scared of things her own size, no matter how many legs they had.

Miss Billie came over to sit with us. When we squeezed up so she could have room, the foxes biting their tails around her shoulder brushed my face. I couldn't believe they were so soft. Their eyes looked wet but they were hard. I could tell without touching. Her clothes smelled sweet and warm.

Miss Billie smoked a cigarette in a long shiny holder. She asked us about this and that and school. I told her we didn't have school now 'cause it was summer, and then her face crinkled again and she started to cry. She said, "I shoulda known. Of course, there's no school."

I said, "Miss Billie, please don't cry." Then Booboo started crying, and I knew old crybaby Chickie would start in, too. I felt bad enough to cry my own self, sitting next to so much sadness. I nudged Chickie for the brown bag, and even though it wasn't three o'clock, I said, "Miss Billie, would you like to join us? We're going to have a bite to eat." I was trying to be polite, but that way of talking always did kill me. Mama would ask folks to stay for a bite, and when they'd finished it was like a meeting of the Clean Plate Club.

Everybody cheered up when Miss Billie said she'd love to. She took off her gloves, long white gloves that flipped out near the elbow. Her fingernails were dark red and shiny. The inside of her arm was purple and lumpy and scary, like it should hurt a lot. But she didn't pay it any mind, and after a minute we didn't either. She reached in and chose the best piece in the bag and smiled like she was happy to be hungry. She didn't chomp into it like we did, biting off more than we could chew. She just pulled strips of white meat and crust off with her fingers and chewed with her red lips close together. Same with the biscuits. She broke off little pieces and placed them neatly in her mouth. I tried to do like her. I even let Chickie have both the wings, though I knew one was for me, but I couldn't see how to eat it in front of her and do it right. Booboo held onto her drumstick until the little dog charmed it out of her. I gave her another one but she was more interested in watching than eating. Me, too.

We had a good time. Miss Billie stayed neat and clean while we got all greasy. When Chickie and Booboo ran to throw the trash in the basket, I asked her how come she'd been crying. She said she didn't know. I asked her how many kids—excuse me, children—she had. She said none. I said she was too pretty to be crying and not have any kids. She said nothing at first, just squeezed me to her side. Then she looked at me close and said, "Don't be like me, sweetheart."

Why not? I knew I was going to be a singer. I wanted to sing at The Green Door like Mama did, like she did. Even my favorite color was the color of the songs she sang, blue. She rode in a fancy car, wore those soft furry foxes around her shoulders, ate the way ladies were supposed to. Why not like her? I didn't say it, I just thought it in my mind.

When the man came and stood over our bench, he didn't say a word, just looked down at Miss Billie. He snapped a leash onto the little dog's collar and started to walk out of the park. Miss Billie gave us each a hug, a kiss, and a dollar. Then she put on her gloves and walked behind the man to The Green Door.

Mama came to get us at four with a smile and a song. "Who's been kissing on my babies?" she said, picking up Booboo, wiping red off her fat little cheek.

"Didn't Miss Billie tell you?" I asked her.

"Tell me what?"

Chickie rushed all in and said, "She was crying, Ma, and everything."

Booboo said, "Doggie, doggie, bow wow."

Mama said, "Bunny, will you please tell me what happened?"

I said, "Nothing. Miss Billie came to our picnic."

"And what else?"

"Nothing else. She just had a bite to eat."